To F

with b

wishes and
many thanks
for what she is.

Yours Ekaterina

MARIA VELEVA
SNEZHANA DANCHEVA—BLAGOEVA

BULGARIAN NATIONAL COSTUMES AND FOLK JEWELLERY

MARIA VELEVA
SNEZHANA DANCHEVA—BLAGOEVA

BULGARIAN NATIONAL COSTUMES AND FOLK JEWELLERY

Translation Marguerite Alexieva

SEPTEMVRI PUBLISHING HOUSE
Sofia

MARIA
VELEVA

BULGARIAN NATIONAL

COSTUMES

СПАСЬ
БОГДАНЬ ХАСН

HISTORICAL DEVELOPMENT

In the diaries, letters, reports and travel notes they have left us, many foreign travellers, who passed through Bulgaria between the 15th and the 19th century (most of them were European diplomats, writers, doctors or scholars), expressed their surprise at and often their admiration of the beauty of Bulgarian national costumes. Their descriptions are eloquent proof of the artistic aspect of traditional Bulgarian costumes. Here are a few quotations taken from such works: '... women, men and children all wear clothes embroidered in silk (1539)'; 'One cannot but mention the jewellery worn by these women. They wear only sleeveless overdresses and chemises, ornamented with much multi-coloured embroidery... However, nothing looked so novel to us as the unusually shaped hats... which gave their wearers weight and an impressive appearance. They are worn in such a way that you think that a Clytemnestra or a Hecuba is entering the stage (1533)'; 'The garments and the beauty of the peasant women in these parts are quite remarkable. They are dressed in white chemises of a thick fabric, but decorated with silks of all hues. They look very trim and beautiful in these garments (1591)'; 'They wear only a chemise and a kind of robe over it. Their hair is braided into plaits, usually with coins woven into them, and hanging down their backs. On their heads they wear little hats, also ornamented; their necklaces are formed of four or five chains (1706)'; 'The freshness of these rose-pickers, their elegant figures and garments, their hair, braided into long plaits falling over their shoulders, the light veils, floating over their heads, so well described by the authors of old (1790); 'Bulgarians plough in garments ornamented with embroidery in wools of different colours. These garments, always very clean, are brilliant and exquisite, particularly in summer, when the embroidery stands out

1

2

on the whiteness of the cotton shirt (1786)'.

The original cut and composition of the garments, the metal jewellery and coins worn with them and the dignity in the bearing of these people encouraged the travellers to sketch them: '... and because the men's garments, as well as those of the women, are the most wonderful thing I saw in this country, I am giving a sketch of them (1621, 1714)'; 'I delayed her with various questions while I sketched the remarkable bridal headdress she wore... the unusually trim garments of a lovely girl, in her blue bolero, held in place by a waistband, her white chemise, as long as a dress, and the ornamentation of her hair, recalled the traditional garments of Gretchen (1865)'.

A variety of data and paintings provide evidence of various kinds about the stability and continuity of the national costumes and their ornamentation in the distant and more recent past; we find them in archaeology, mural paintings, in manuscripts, even in language, but particularly so in ethnography.

Some of the most interesting sources of our knowledge on the subject of national costumes are the illustrations of mediaeval manuscripts and church books of the 12th to 14th century, both Bulgarian and foreign. Along with the costumes of feudal rulers and nobles, with their insignia, regal attributes and ornaments, along with battle scenes we find Bulgarian mediaeval costumes worn by the population in the Middle Ages in town and country

1

Donor portraits in Kremikovtsi Monastery, Sofia, 1493.

2

Donor portraits in the Church of Bachkovo Monastery, 1643.

3

3
Judgement Day (part of a Fresco), in Bachkovo Monastery. Painted by Zahari Zograph in 1840.

they are graceful and intricate, and particularly rich in colour.
A comparison of the forms, components, woven and embroidered decoration of the Bulgarian costumes and the jewellery worn with them depicted in the mural paintings of donors in churches and monasteries (for instance, in Boyana Church, 1259, Zemen Monastery, the 14th century Church in the village of Kalotino, Kremikovtsi Monastery, 1493), as well as in the genre scenes (the frescoes in Hrelyo's Tower at Rila Monastery) shows the same elements in the traditional costumes which survived into the early twentieth century and we even find great similarity in them. This allows us to think that the artistic qualities of Bulgarian national costumes are rooted in far earlier periods of history.
As to the folk-singer who, at all times, expressed the people's aesthetic sense, he incessantly praises the intransient beauty of Bulgarian national costumes. His poetic description of a Bulgarian costume, shows all the marvellous beauty and charm of Nature which according to the Bulgarian people, is the richest and clearest source of beauty. The garments are usually compared with the colours of garden or wild flowers: the chemise is as white as a 'white rose'; the *soukman* (sleeveless overdress) is as blue as 'a pansy'; the skirt is as yelow as 'the little crocus'; while in certain songs it is even said that all the separate garments are made of flowers: 'a *manofil* (a woman's summer outer garment) made of white poppies'; 'a shirt made of a hollyhock'; 'a head scarf of

nasturtium'; 'a waistband of red roses'; 'a white *saya* (sleeveless wrap-over overdress) of white hollyhock'; and so on. The ornamentation on the fabrics, according to the folk-singer, reflects the brilliance of the heavenly bodies. For instance, in his words, a woman's chemise has shining on it 'on the breast– the clear sun; on the shoulders – the clear moon, on the skirts – nothing but starlets, on the sleeves, only morning stars'. They are distinguished by the dynamic expressiveness of the natural elements. Thus, in movement the skirts of a woman's garment 'sough like the wind through a forest' or like 'the winds of the Pirin Mountains'; the *soukman* unfolds like 'a dark cloud', the metal jewellery 'shines like the ice on the Danube'. They seem to be full of the vitality of the animal world. For instance, the embroidery on the man's shirt stands out like 'a falcon's eyes', 'a peacock's feathers', 'a bird's wings with speckled feathers'. Sometimes some parts of the garments are compared to musical instruments – the 'little apron' is compared in charm to a 'little violin'. Even the quiver of a piece of jewellery can touch the most delicate cords of a human soul with its artistic effect, it can make a man tremble – a 'lad's heart' trembles for a 'lass's white face' like 'little butterflies tremble'.

According to the aesthetic sense of the people, a costume should be modelled after 'the laws of beauty' so that the art put into its making should bring even inanimate objects to life, like the 'living

4

Transporting the Relics of St. John of Rila (Part of a mural in Orlitsa Metoh near Rila Monastery). Painted by Nikola Ivanov Obrazopissov in 1863.

4

water' in the fairy stories. Bulgarian women from various parts of the country have been known to say that 'clothes should be so lovely that even if you were to dress a piece of wood in them it would become beautiful'. What better synthesis of the people's aesthetic ideal of clothing can you have? Again according to the folksinger, a bride's costume should make her look so beautiful that when she passes through a forest 'a dry tree should bring forth leaves' and 'the dry leaves should only look withered'; while when she enters the church 'the icons should speak'. Sometimes the people even exaggerate the artistic effect of the costums, saying that with her beauty and the brilliance of her garments a lass can surpass the beauty of the heavenly bodies; 'The clear sun shines on three mountains and six flocks, but the little lass shines on six mountains with nine flocks.' Even the heavenly body itself acknowledges that a beautifully dressed lass is a 'a sun on earth – on earth among people, and in the green grass.

The artistic qualities of the Bulgarian national costumes are also due to the ethnic elements which brought them into being and which played a part in forming the Bulgarian nationality. Slav elements are also found in them; at the turn of the fifth and sixth centuries these tribes began to settle in the lands of the future Bulgarian State which was founded in 681. This State developed and grew strong after this date. The Slav origin, character and aspect of the Bulgarian national costumes are apparent in one of

5

5
Part of a mural in Arapovo Monastery. Painted by Georgi Danchov in 1864.

6

7

their principal features– their decoration, shown also in the terminologyof the garments,their parts and accessories. Whole sets of costumes generally Slav in character, and found wherever Slavs had settled, show the early advance and high level of culture in the garments worn by these tribes. Thes also show that the Bulgarians inherited from them a well-developed system of apparel, with great artistic qualities for the Early Middle Ages.
The Slav aspect of traditional Bulgarian garb was maintained, intensified and renewed because of the uninterrupted contacts of the Bulgarian people with other Slav peoples right down to our own day.

6
Woman's festive costume from Gabrovo. Early 20th century. Painted by Ivan Mrkvička.

7
Embroidered end of a head scarf worn with a *sokai* in Gabrovo. Early 19th century.

However, the Thracians, settled in the Balkan Peninsula long before the Slavs or Bulgarians appeared there, had been in constant contact with Greece and the Mediterranean civilization. Inevitably Slavs and Bulgarians were influenced through them by this ancient civilization and by the Byzantine civilization which inherited it. Among the elements in Slav and Bulgarian costumes, which can be traced to Thrace and Greece, are the textiles, locally produced, and suitable to local conditions of work and way of life. In fact, traditional Bulgarian costumes were influenced by the numerous peoples with whom the position of their land – a crossroads between East and West, North and South – put them in touch. Despite these influences there were always specific features in the costumes worn by the Bulgarians and they undoubtedly played a part in strengthening the Bulgarian nationality. There are elements in the traditional Bulgarian costumes which are Proto-Bulgarian in character, according to the researches of ethnographers and art historians. However, few Proto-Bulgarian words have been left in the language of the Bulgarian people (the

8

8

Woven end of a head scarf worn with the *sokai* to form a woman's headdress. Early 19th century.

name of their nationality, 'Bulgarian', is one of them); because of the important part played by the Proto-Bulgarians in founding and organizing the Bulgarian State, there are a number of features in the people's traditional garb which were obviously inherited from these ancestors and their culture.

A retrospective analysis of the elements of traditional Bulgarian clothing in the pre-national period leads to the conclusion that it was close to the cultural level of the various ethnic groups met with when the period of late Antiquity was waning, and the Early Middle Ages were dawning. These ethnic groups took part in form ing the Bulgarian nationality.

The Slav modifications of parts of costumes, and of other whole costumes, together with their decorative elements and techniques, considered as inherited from the Proto-Bulgarians and the Thracians, can be accepted as an indication of Slav predominance in the process of forming the Bulgarian culture.

Inhabiting, as they did, a land which was a crossroads between East and West, North and South, the Bulgarians came into direct or indirect contact with many peoples because of the synchronic and diachronic link between them; they therefore underwent many influences and borrowed much from these peoples in their costumes. Certain features of the garb of Ancient Hellas to be found in Bulgarian costumes can be attributed to the association of the Bulgarians with the Ancient Mediterranean world, and its peoples, who were their neighbours and who formed the local Balkan population.

Bulgarian national costumes were at a comparatively high level in the early stages of their development and this is due to the strong impact of the Late Greek and Early Byzantine civilizations, which enriched the experience and artistic skill of the Bulgarians in

9

10

technology and production, without hindering them from expressing their ethnic character. Bulgarian culture can be considered as having played the part of a link between the Old World and the New,which later influenced the development of European culture and art.

In certain details, insignificant at first sight, local varieties of the costumes show traces of the cultural history of theBulgarian lands, with influences and borrowings from various tribes and peoples with whom the Bulgarians were in contact in the early periods of this history; these traces are faint by now.

From this amalgam of inheritance,borrowings and influences the Bulgarian people managed, through their own creative impulses, to create a national garb, unique in its ethnic features. A historical review of Bulgarian costumes, compared with those of other Slav and Balkan peoples, shows a great degree of independence in their development, although the Slav and Balkan peoples received the same heritage and developed under very similar geographical and economic conditions. The whole system of features of a utilitarian, technical and artistic nature, which mark Bulgarian costumes and which no other peoples could repeat, are inherent in the eventful period in which the Bulgarian State was formed and the Bulgarian nationality became firmly established; this was a process which lasted without interruption during the country's whole history. The development of Bulgarian traditional clothing brings confirmation of the conclusions drawn from the cultural history of the country, which show that the Bulgarian nationality developed not only as an ethnic and political unit, but also as a cultural community. The uniquely national originality of these costumes shows that in the Middle Ages the Bulgarian lands were a creative centre independent of other peoples and countries in

9
Woman's festive costume from Veliko Turnovo region. Early 19th century. Painted by Ivan Dimitrov.

10
Girl's spring costume from Troyan region. End of 19th century.

11

11

11

11
Embroidery on the sleeve of a woman's chemise. Troyan region. End of 19th century.

many respects. The differentiation of the national aspect of Bulgarian costumes as regards forms, components, entire composition and decoration, is visual proof of the people's strongly expressed independent creative activity. Written sources, even as early as the early feudal period show that Bulgarian clothing took shape at a time when the national name *Bulgarians* appeared and took its place, and nothing can be more eloquent of the manner in which the nationally specific features of Bulgarian culture had become clearly marked.

The development of certain Bulgarian costumes marks periods of interaction between the Balkan peoples during the Middle Ages and even somewhat later, periods in which the Bulgarian people took part on an equal footing with others in creating cultural values, or in exchanging them as fullfledged partners with other peoples. However, the national character of a number of elements of a practical, and more particularly of an artistic nature, indicate that the achievements of other peoples were refracted in an entirely independent way in the creative work of the Bulgarian people; that they were determined by the local features of their social, political, economic and cultural development.

In their steady march to more advanced forms, these elements were included within the cultural process of feudal Bulgaria, in manifestations, which are recognized as the beginnings of an Eastern European Renaissance. Elements and signs typical of the artistic style of the garments worn in the Early Renaissance, but originally used in accordance with their own aesthetic norms, are to be found even in the ethnic features of a number of varieties of Bulgarian costumes, and particularly of those which serve as the foundation of the development of national costumes of an urban type in the period of the Bulgarian National Revival. Bulgarian

12
Embroidery on the sleeve of a woman's chemise. Troyan region . End of 19th century.

13
Shepherd's costume from Troyan region. Early 20th century.

12

13

national clothing does not appear to have been subjected to mediaeval fashions. Probably the sound vitality of the Bulgarian people, the lifegiving principle in the world outlook of the ordinary 'real man' about a man's ideal image, particularly the ideal image of a woman, maintained even during the Middle Ages features to which a Renaissance character is attributed.

With its vividly expressed specifically national features, mainly apparent in its artistic form, Bulgarian national clothing became a powerful weapon in the struggle to maintain the national consciousness and the struggle for national liberation during the periods of foreign domination (the 11th to 12th, and the 15th to 20th centuries). Data obtained from different sources – the potraits of donors (16th, 17th, 18th centuries and the first decades of the 19th century) and from various periods of Bulgarian history, notes in travel books, documents, etc., show that the garments they wore were some of the expressive ethno-differentiating features which determined the Bulgarian nationality and that at the same time it integrated the Bulgarian population ethnically within the boundaries of the Bulgarian lands. Unity in principle, as regards the ethnical features of the forms in which Bulgarian costumes crystallized as early as the Middle Ages, shows that the ethnic relations between the population of different regions of the country were maintained not only by similar historical, social, economic and geographic conditions, but also by the the far-reaching historical and cultural relations, which were not broken even during the most eventful vicissitudes of the nation's destiny; even under strong assimilating oppression and national discrimination; even when, in the epoch of Ottoman rule, it became necessary for political or economic reasons for the po-

14
Embroidery on the sleeve of a woman's chemise. Troyan region. End of 19th century.

14

15

16

pulation to leave the country and to spend several centuries in foreign parts (the Bulgarians in Asia Minor, in the Banat, etc.). The picture of the garments worn in the country changed in quality during one of the most glorious periods in Bulgarian history, a period of an eventful economic and cultural advance, when the struggle for liberation began – the period of the National Revival. This period began in a particularly striking way in the first years of the 18th century. New costumes came into being in response to the heightened demands of labour, life, culture, aesthetics, the community, etc.

The traditional principles, which governed the designing, structure and modelling of Bulgarian costumes, traditions that were almost unaffected by time, continued to be in force in the National Revival period.

However, in this period there were already signs of adapting them to more modern clothing, more suitable to changing conditions. The division of labour appeared; craftsmen were no longer engaged in farming and stockbreeding; production and marketing were not in the same hands; women who were engaged in producing marketable wares were no longer exclusively engaged in housework; all these changes rid the traditional costumes worn by Bulgarians of those elements which were suitable for the work of ploughmen, shepherds, harvesters and weavers, and brought them into line with the new conditions of their new activities. A

15

Girl's festive costume , worn when dancing Lazar Dances in the Spring. Karnobat region. Early 20th century.

16

Head dress on Lazarki worn in Karnobat region. Early 20th century.

17

17
Girls from Karnobat region in the costumes worn for the Lazar Dances. Early 20th century.

craftsman was able to wear garments made of finer fabrics in different colours, more voluminous and better cut; he was more affluent and could afford outer garments of fine homespun or cloth, usually dark blue, and ornamented with black braid, silk stripes and furs; in cut, these garments were much wider particularly the *potouri* , a type of full-bottomed breeches; waistbands, handkerchiefs and other accessories made of imported silks, usually brought from the East, were worn; the sheepskin hat was replaced by a cylindrical hat of black fur, sometimes astrakhan; the pigskin sandals were replaced by leather shoes, sewn or made with wooden pegs. Over this costume a long, wide, furlined coat was worn; these new garments replaced the old costumes, made of rough homespun in the natural colour of the wool, cut to make them convenient for work in the fields and the pastures, and the men no longer wore the mushroomshaped sheepskin hats,or the *yamourlouk,* the heavy flared and hooded cape which kept the shepherds warm and dry in all weathers.

The garments worn by Bulgarians in the National Revival period also show the improvements introduced by a better use of natural energy: water was used to run fulling mills; this improved the quality of the homespuns used for outer garments: they became thicker, wore better, and were also softer; their surfaces had a sheen. At the same time braid looms began to be used at the end of the 18th century, and particularly in the first decades of the

19th century. Braid was now used to ornament outer woollen garments; the *potouri,* waistcoats and *abi* (coats) worn by the men, the boleros, *soukmans, klashniks* (long coats) and *mentés* (short jackets) worn by the women.

The development of the crafts in the National Revival period was apparent in new elements, which enriched the clothes worn by Bulgarians. As the products of these crafts found larger markets in the Ottoman Empire, trade increased, and in the centres whose economy had improved, foreign fabrics, decorative elements and jewellery began to be worn, particularly on festive occasions.

The Bulgarian people considered their clothing from a utilitarian point of view, but they also made aesthetic demands on it; this provided a favourable climate for the Renaissance principles apparent in the costumes they wore in the National Revival period, principles which were not bound by any feudal ideology or religious dogmatism.

The aesthetic demands on their clothing made in the Middle Ages by the ordinary Bulgarians, with their love of life, had less to do with their sense of possession than with their sense of beauty;this was satisfied by the synthesis in them of the various branches of decorative art. These demands remained a lasting feature in the aesthetic sense of the National Revival Bulgarians, though adapted at that period to new forms, corresponding to the economic demands of production and the new way of life. The new upper and outer garments, continued to be ornamented, as the folk-singer has it with: 'as many stars as there are in the sky, so many patterns on the furlined coat, as many leaves in the forest, so much braiding on the waistcoat' (Trun); while the women of Sofia and Ochrid who wore these garments looked as if

18
Festive girl's costume worn for the spring Lazar Dances in Sliven region. End of the 19th century.

19
Girls' and bachelors' costumes from Sliven region. End of the 19th century.

20
Elderly woman's everyday costume. Sliven region. End of 19th century.

18

19

20

21
Apron from Sliven region. End of 19th century.

22
Festive summer costume worn by young women in Sliven region. Early 20th century.

23
Young woman's spring costume. Sliven region. Early 20th century.

they were 'dressed in the sun, belted by the moon and had small stars on their shoulders.'

Exaggerated ornamentation of the garments in the Middle Ages and in the National Revival period obviously affected their quality and not their quantity, and the striving was to achieve a highly artistic effect.

The clothing of Bulgarian women in the National Revival period showed the stability of a characteristic feature in the development of Bulgarian national culture: the conscious avoidance of a stifling atmosphere of stagnation, of restricting and isolating oneself from the rest of world. In this period horizons were widened; people were no longer shut into their own region alone; economic and cultural relations with different countries and peoples increased, and the Bulgarian women chose from among them the elements and features which were progressive and democratic, but only adopted them after they had adapted them to their own taste and requirements.

This process of renewal in the garments worn by Bulgarians in the National Revival period began and developed most intensively in the towns, where the most essential results were obtained, and where it was stimulated by intensive social, economic and cultural activities; this renewal gradually spread to the villages which were in touch with the large centres owing to their social and economic relations.

In the National Revival period clothing was part of the process which formed the national culture and national consciousness. It showed the strong link between the national culture then being formed and the folk culture which had preceded it; an unbroken continuity in the course of the long and complex process of its creation was proved, costumes being rooted in the traditions of

21

22

23

24

25

26

the masses. The appearance and formation of these costumes showed the lines along which the Bulgarian nationality was coming to the fore.

In present-day Bulgaria now that a single material and technical base has been created and the ethnographic regions are being effaced, it is natural that garments should be created to satisfy the growing utilitarian and aesthetic demands of the working people. The rich heritage of national costumes plays the part of an inexhaustible source of models for modern decorative art, the art crafts and even industry today. The intransient beauty of this cultural heritage does much for the aesthetic and patriotic education of the whole community, particularly of the growing generations. The use of this heritage maintains the national features of the new socialist culture.

A review of the development of Bulgarian national clothing shows that in the course of its centuries of existence it has been subjected to one of the most important traits of social development-historical continuity. It was incessantly formed in harmony with the life of the working people in all its aspects, and this has been the principal motive force in its steady progress.

24
Young man's festive costume from Sliven region. End of 19th century.

25
Embroidery on the sleeve of a man's shirt. Sliven region. End of 19th century.

26
Shepherd's costume from Sliven region. End of 19th century.

28

27

27

Shepherd's costume from Sliven region. Early 20th century.

28

Festive woman's costume worn in the town of Kotel in the National Revival period. Mid-19th century.

29

30

29
Festive costume worn by the Karakachani, Wallachian nomad shepherds, in Sliven region. Early 20th century.

30
Festive women's costumes from Sliven region. Early 19th century.

31
Head scarves as worn on festive occasions with head jewellery from Yambol region. End of the 19th century.

32
Head dress and jewellery worn by a young woman from Yambol region. Late 19th century.

33
Festive women's costumes from Yambol region. Early 20th century.

34
Embroidery of the hem of a *soukman,* Yambol region. Late 19th century.

31

32

33

34

35

36

37

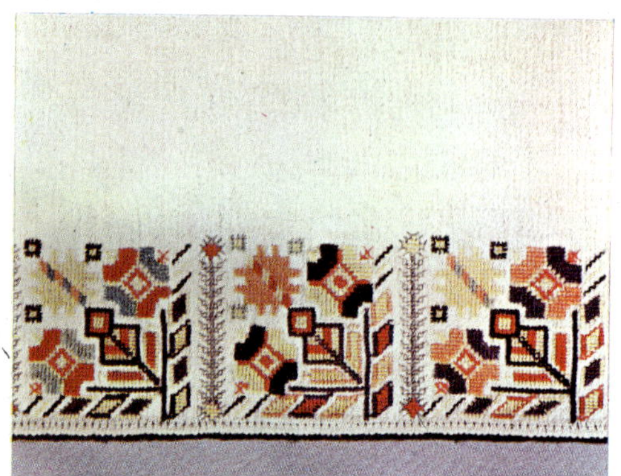

38

39

40

14

42

35
Woman's costume from Elhovo region. Early 20th century.

36
Koledari (carol singers) from Elhovo region. Early 20th century.

37
Embroidery around the hem of a woman's chemise from Elhovo region. Late 19th century.

38 39
Embroidery around the hem of a woman's chemise. Elhovo region. Late 19th century.

40
Apron from Elhovo region. Late 19th century.

41
Apron from Elhovo region. Late 19th century.

42
Embroidery around the front opening of a *soukman* from Elhovo. Late 19th century.

MATERIALS AND WAYS OF PREPARING THEM

Besides their very specific character, and the essential features of Bulgarian culture inherent in them, Bulgarian national costumes owe their beauty to the people's creative and artistic sense. Textiles are, naturally, the principal material, woven or knitted, and embroidery by way of ornamentation. The fabrics were all hand woven, and only after the crafts and industry developed were factory-made fabrics used to a limited extent. Woollen fabrics predominated, which were used for upper and outer garments; stockings were hand-knitted. In the mountainous regions of the Balkan Range, the Sredna Gora Mountains, etc., even the shirts worn by shepherds and lumbermen were made of woollen fabrics, to protect them from the cold of winter. However, hempen and linen fabrics were also extensively used, as a tradition inherited from Thracians and Slavs, and also because flax and hemp grow well in the country. Silk was also used in olden times, chiefly by way of ornamentation. In more recent times, mainly the second half of the 19th century, and the early 20th century, silk replaced wool in many fabrics, whole garments being fashioned for men and for women out of silk fabrics. Cotton was introduced comparatively much later, being imported as a fabric and as yarns; somewhat later still the peasants began to grow it in suitable regions of the country, and to spin it.

Textiles were sometimes made of only one material, and sometimes of mixtures, according to the use to which they were put. Fabrics used for aprons or short skirts in North-Western Bulgaria were woven with a hempen or cotton warp of highly twisted yarn, so that it would be able to stand up to the tension of the stretching during weaving; fine woollen yarns were used for the weft, to obtain a thick fabric, which would be quite stiff and in which the warp would be so well covered as not to

43

44

show through. In other cases textile materials of different origins and processing were mixed, to give the fabric elasticity, relief, or a crêpe surface, as well as other utilitarian and more particularly artistic qualities. For outer working garments, wool and goat's hair were mixed, to make them waterproof.

The old traditions of processing materials for fabrics used by the Bulgarians and particularly by Bulgarian women are well illustrated in the picture painted of them by travellers, whether foreign or our own, a picture, which was essentially the same in different epochs. They describe women as perpetually having a distaff in their hands or thrust into their waistbands, and spinning even when they are walking along, and this picture was to be seen well on into the 20th century. An English traveller wrote in 1827: 'This simple machine supplies the whole family with clothes.' Another foreigner in 1597 praised Bulgarian women for being 'so industrious in sprinning that when they walk along the streets you cannot see them without work, but they put a distaff in their waistbands and spin as they walk along.' This picture of the Bulgarian woman seems to be closely linked with the picture of the Thracian woman of olden times in the Bulgarian lands who, according to the description of a fifth century B.C. writer, was to be seen 'with a water jar on her head, leading the horse to be watered with one hand and spinning flax with the other.'

Various techniques of weaving were used from the most primitive

43
Elderly spinner from Groudovo region. Early 20th century.

44
Woman's costume from Nova Zagora region. Early 20century.

45
Ends of women's waistbands from Kazanluk region. Late 19th century.

46
Women's costumes from Strara Zagora region. Early 20th century.

to the most intricate, always with a view to the practical and the artistic qualities of the fabrics, and the possibilities offered by the primitive wooden loom. The multi-coloured belts and strips, with flat, round or square cross sections, were worked in a manner which was a transition from knitting to weaving. The multi-coloured and richly ornamented belts worn by women were primitively woven in a technique called *na kori,* the *kori* (bark) being small wooden square with a hole in each corner, through which the threads were passed; they facilitated the handling of threads, which were twisted so that a fabric rather like a knitted one was obtained, while the pattern was formed by a chain of motifs of different shapes and colours. Multi-coloured belts were woven on a loom without a reed. The basket and the quadruple weave are the most widespread, with two and four heddles each, worked horizontally on a domestic loom. Various methods and devices were used to obtain fabrics of different practical and artistic quality: with an even or compact weave smooth or slightly raised, with a fluffy, tufted or fringed surface, fine and transparent or thick and stiff fabrics, etc., each of which had its special use. The rich ornamentation of the fabrics used for garments was obtained by combining basic weaving techniques with others, some of which were very primitive, such as that of *kussané,* weaving coloured threads by hand into the weft, when the threads of the warp are separated or 'open', a multi-coloured but smooth surface being thus obtained; Bulgarian women also mastered new and intricate weaving techniques, for instance, weaving with numerous heddles, with the help of which they were also able to weave modern patterns and various other fabrics. Knitting, another branch of textile production, had a far more restricted but exactly defined use in costumes. Stockings, *kaltsi* (a kind of gaiters), *narukvitsi* (arm-covers worn from wrist to elbow), gloves and mittens were knitted. To these should be added the different ties for aprons, belts and waistbands. In their striving to create beautiful garments Bulgarian women even used the seams as decorative elements, crocheting or sewing them along the edges, ornamenting them with needle-point lace, usually in silk, fashioning delicate little figures, like those of the *kenés* (needle-point lace edgings and nets). In more recent times knitting has replaced fabrics to a considerable extent in the costums, particularly as regards upper garments.

Furs have a comparatively small place in traditional Bulgarian costumes. A sheepskin jacket, called *kozhouh,* was used as an outer garment chiefly in the cold mountainous regions. It was worn with the fur inside and was usually left in its natural colour, but was often decorated by appliquéing coloured leather strips and embroidery. The man's hat known as a *kalpak* or *gougla,* was made all over the country from sheep or lamb skins and rarely, quite exceptionally, of goatskin, always with the fur on the out-

47
Festive costume of a girl, who is to take part in the spring dances on Lazarus Day. Plovdiv region. Late 19th century.

48
Headdress of a *Lazarka,* taking part in the spring dances. Plovdiv region. Late 19th century.

47

48

side, and usually in the dark, natural colour. Leather was used for footwear, pigskin or oxskin, from which *tsarvouli* (sandals), slippers and shoes were made. Men's belts of different widths, straps for holding puttees in place, straps for bags, carried over the shoulder, for carrying food to work, etc., were made of worked and ornamented leather. The custom of wearing leather garments in performing certain rituals (the garments worn on such occasions were usually archaic) and at weddings also in certain regions, such as that of Sofia, indicates a period when fur and leather garments were worn by the Bulgarians, but this period is long past. Metal – silver, gold, copper, bronze and various alloys – was only used in making jewellery, some of which was initially only practical in use, such as belt buckles, the belts themselves made of small metal plaques threaded onto a leather strip; hair-pins, buttons, used to hold the edges of garments together, but they all became decorative elements and were artistically worked.

Traditional Bulgarian costumes show a fairly high level of technology in the making. Almost all the garments were sewn, but in cut and shape they conformed to the structure of the body; they were richly and suitably ornamented. These elements show a comparatively early advance in the making of Bulgarian popularly worn garments, and a transition to more cultural forms, as well as improvements in making them. The presence of certain articles of apparel which were not sewn in some regions – such as the back

49
Costume of a *sourvakar*, worn on New Year's Day, when accomplishing a fertility rite. Plovdiv region. Late 19th century.

50
Young woman's costume from Karlovo, Late 19th century.

49

50

51

52

skirts in the two-apron costume of Northern Bulgaria, or the aprons worn with most women's costumes – is explained by the practical purpose in certain work, or by their role as decorative elements. In some cases they were even the central decorative element in the costume, a function performed by aprons in many local costumes, such as those in the Sliven, Yambol and the Central Rhodope districts. The general trend of a definite form in garments is apparent even in these unsewn garments, because of the decorative framework around them, or the pleats or gathers used on them. Bulgarian women made the clothes of the family and showed a thorough knowledge of the fabrics they had at their disposal, and a fine aesthetic taste in ornamenting them. They were also very well versed in the art of dyeing, and in the past, before the introduction of aniline dyes, only used the natural dyes obtained from plants. The range of colours and shades they worked with was responsible for the beauty of the patterns they embroidered. What is more, their colours did not fade. Aside from vegetable dyes, a few of animal origin were used, such as crimson, cochineal and sepia. Certain minerals were also used, and other substances, adapted for use as dyes, such as lime and soot. In their 'laboratories' these women, who were artists and chemists too in their daily life, used many different substances of organic origin to set their colours, and by prolonging or shortening the time during which their yarns or textiles were kept in the dye, and often by

51
Women's costumes from Svilengrad region. Early 20th century.

52
Young woman's festive costume from Smolyan region. Second half of the 19th century.

53

54

53
Women's festive costumes from Smolyan region. Second half of the 19th century.

54
Young woman's festive costume from Smolyan region. Late 19th century.

'secret' processes, managed to obtain a great variety of shades in the same colour. Between 300 and 400 different formulas for dyeing are known to have been used by these simple Bulgarian women, intent upon making the clothes their family wore as lovely as possible.

The traditional costumes showed that the people had an extensive knowledge of the practical and sanitary qualities of the fabrics they used, being well aware of the degree to which each of them was loosely enough woven to allow the free circulatin of air, steam and heat; which were hygroscopic, and which allowed rapid evaporation. This knowledge led them to adopt linen for the summer clothes worn during harvesting, because it quickly absorbs moisture, thus cooling the skin; linen was made in a fairly loose weave. Because of their warmth supple woollen fabrics were chosen for upper garments in the mountains to protect their wearers from snow and rain. And because goat's hair is resistant to water, it was added to the yarns from which the garments worn by shepherds were made.

The great variety to be found in national costumes is due to the fact that fabrics were produced in the home and that producer and consumer were one and the same person; this is also responsible for the beauty and variety of designs used to ornament the costumes. This variety was maintained even after craftsmen took over a large part of the manufacture of national costumes. At

55

56

56

first such work was given to women noted for their skill, and who were known to keep to the local traditional patterns. They replaced the travelling craftsmen and journeymen, who also preserved local traditions and took personal tastes into account. In this way a degree of similarity was introduced into the garments worn in the villages, and later spread to larger regions. Craftsmen played a greater part in making clothes for the townspeople, but they were limited to upper and outer garments, particularly the latter.

55
Young bride's costume, Smolyan region. Second half of the 19th century.

56
Women's costumes of Bulgarian settlers in Asia Minor. Early 20th century.

57

58

57
Bagpipe player from Smolyan region. Early 20th century.

58
Men's *horo* from Smolyan region. Early 20th century.

59

60

61

59
Girls wearing festive costumes. Ihtiman region. Early 20th century.

60
Girl's costume from Ihtiman region. Early 20th century.

61
Costume worn by girl engaged to be married. Ihtiman region. Early 20th century.

62

62

62
Embroidery around the hem of woman's chemise. Ihtiman region. Mid-19th century.

STRUCTURE AND COMPOSITION

A detailed analysis of Bulgarian national costumes shows that in material, cut, form, structure, complete composition and even decoration they are adapted to the basic labours of the Bulgarians; the nature of theirfeaturesshow that they are, above all, working clothes. The old costumes are adapted to the principal means of livelihood of the Bulgarians in the past: farming, stockbreeding and partly the crafts. The fabrics of which they were made were, in the nature of the textiles used, their treatment and colour, resistant to atmospheric conditions in work out in the open; their cut, allowing freedom of movement to a ploughman and a shepherd; their structure, allowing themselves to be adapted to definite working conditions; their composition, adapted to the structure of the body and the demands of hygiene – all these features show that work was one of the principal factors in shaping the garb of the Bulgarians. The man's costume, consisting of a knee-length shirt with fairly wide skirts, worn with a waistband, which continued its existence for the longest time in Northern Bulgaria and the Pirin region, and the women's two-apron costume, which held sway for the longest time in the Danubian Plain, are recognized in ethnography as garments chiefly suitable for farm work. Their use is connected with hard work in the fields at various seasons of the year. On the northern slopes of Stara Planina (the Balkan Range) two types of women's costumes were worn – the two apron and the *soukman* types; the former, being lighter, was worn during work in the fields in spring and summer, while the *soukman* was put on after the harvest has been brought in. In the grain-producing Danubian Plain, and in the fertile valleys of the Rivers Strouma and Mesta, the farmers wore a costume consisting of a long shirt, worn over close-fitting trousers all summer long, and in winter it was changed for one in which the trousers were the main feature. Shepherds, on the other hand, chiefly wore clothes made of thick, warm fabrics, often waterproof, with a fluffy surface; the costume had a fairly complex structure, and even had constant accessories, such as a *yamourlouk* (cape) and a shawl, which could serve as a blanket. This costume, worn by the shepherds in the Rhodopes, the Pirin Mountains and Stara Planina, was eminently suitable for work out in the open under unfavourable conditions. The costumes worn by the craftsmen, who had come to the fore as affluent men in the National Revival period, were also connected with their work and way of life. A guild member, whose work was done in the closed work-shop, could afford to wear garments made of finer fabrics, which fitted him more closely and could be dyed black or dark blue and be more richly ornamented. Shirts made of fine cotton or silk fabrics, upper garments of blue or black homespun or cloth, a bright red woollen waistband, the pleated *potouri* (full-bottomed breeches), a short and narrow jacket trimmed with fur, and rich braiding, formed the costume worn by the craftsmen. As to the women of the Sredna Gora region, Stara Planina, the Rila and Pirin Mountains, and other centres of the National Revival, they were now included in manufacture, particularly in textiles, and replaced the two-apron, *soukman* and *saya* costumes they had worn until then and which were suitable for work in the fields and in the house, with skirts and dresses which met the demands of the new way of life and labour conditions as producers of goods.

A detailed and thorough study of folk costumes shows that even details on them, which are insignificant at first sight, owe their existence to labour conditions. Aprons and the way they were worn with some Western Rhodope costumes either in front or to

63

Girl from Samokov region. Late 19th century. Painted by Ivan Mrkvička.

64

Embroidery on the sleeve of a woman's chemise. Samokov region. Late 19th century.

65

Embroidery on a *soukman* and jewellery from Samokov region. Late 19th century

63

64

65

66
Embroidery on the sleeve of a woman's chemise, Samokov region. Second half of the 19th century.

67
Embroidery of the sleeve of a woman's chemise. Samokov region. Second half of the 19th century.

68
Embroidery on the sleeve of a woman's chemise. Samokov region. Second half of the 19th century.

69
Embroidery on the sleeve of a woman's chemise. Samokov region. Second half 19th century.

70 71
Embroidery on the sleeve of a woman's chemise. Samokov region Mid-19th century.

72
Embroidery on the hem of a woman's chemise. Samokov region. Mid-19th century.

73
Embroidery around the hem of woman's chemise. Samokov region. Mid-19th century.

74
Embroidery around the hem of a woman's chemise. Samokov region. Mid–19th century.

66

67

68

69

70

71

72

74

73

75

76

one side, clearly show that their initial purpose was to keep the garments from wear and soiling. The knee-pieces on men's narrow trousers were placed on them for the same reason, to strengthen that part of the garment which would wear out most quickly in farm work or animal husbandry.

However, in the course of time the initial purpose of these elements was gradually masked by the artistic form which the people gave them, so that it would please their taste.

Called into existence by purely practical needs, garments most often became decorative elements, because of the beautifully shaped edgings, braiding and embroideries worked on them. These elements, of clothing, initially purely practical in intention, becoming ornamental only later, are among the most striking indications of the incessant urge of the Bulgarians to achieve beauty; they also show their creative ability and skilful work.

Each costume had numerous variants, adapted to work under special conditions. Even the simplest costume worn by a farmer – the long white shirt worn loose over the trousers, underwent changes at different times. When ploughing was the order of the day, the shirt was worn with the right or left end tucked into the waistband so that it would not get in the way of a ploughman's movements. The sower, on the other hand, in many parts of the country, particularly in the South, always wore an apron as a necessary accessory, to keep his clothes clean. The shepherd's costume, when he was out with his flock in plain or forest, was not to be thought of without a red or white shawl, as in the Rhodopes and the Pirin mountains, or without a tufted blanket and *yamourlouk* in the plains of Thrace or Sofia; he had to have a wide waistband in the folds of which he put not only his personal belongings, but also the instruments he needed when his sheep

75
Embroidery on the sleeve of a woman's chemise. Stankedimitrovo region. First half of the 19th century.

76
Embroidery on the sleeve of a woman's chemise. Stankedimitrovo region. Late 19th century.

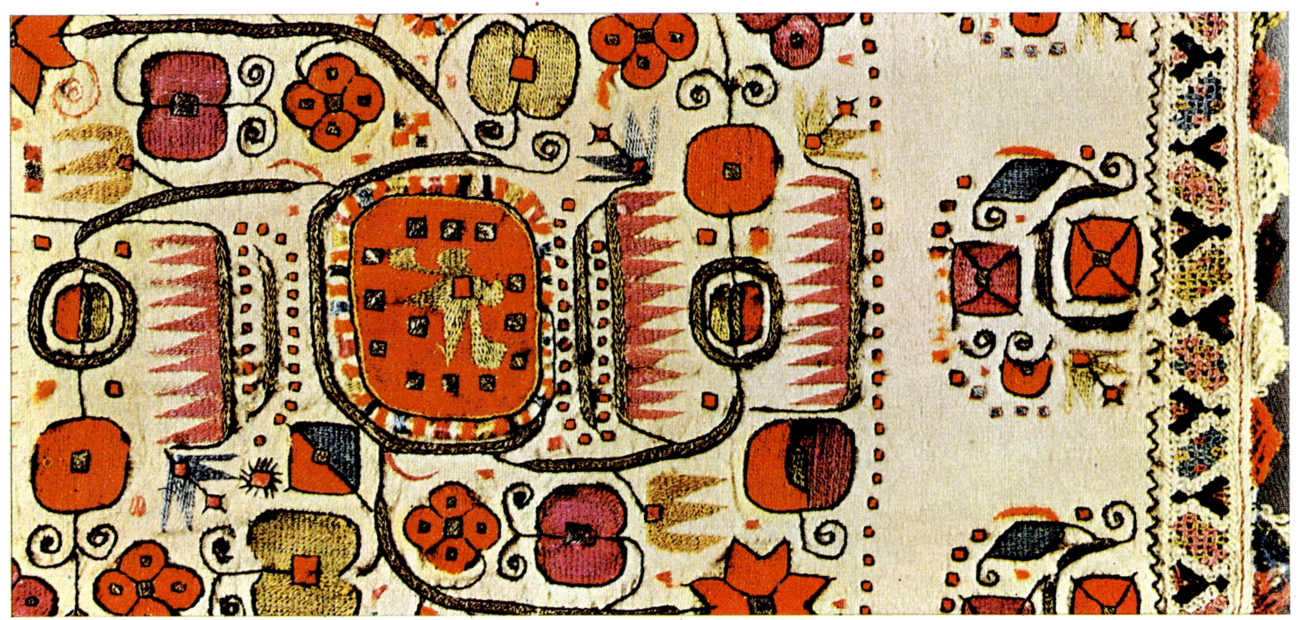

77

77
Embroidery on the sleeve of a woman's chemise. Stankedimitrovo region Late 20th century.

were sick; some food, to tempt them with and his inseparable musical instruments. The costumes worn by craftsmen also showed variants,depending on theconditions of their work; these were apparent in the wuality of the fabrics from which they wre made, the colour, details and cut. A builder did not wear the same costume as a coppersmith, for the same reasons. A builder worked out in the open, like a shepherd, so his costume was quite like that worn by shepherds; while a coppersmith could allow himself clothes made of finer homespun in dark colours.

Women's costumes showed particularly great adaptability to different kinds of work. A striking example of this is the way the apron was worn in an ordinary costume, depending on the work being done. In field and household work the two-apron and *saya* costumes seemed to acquire wings – edges of their front skirts were pinned back so as not to hinder movement. As already mentioned, even the hair-do conformed to the requirement not to hamper work. The way the headscarf was worn was also adapted to labour conditions. In Lovech district, when harvesting was at its height, the women tied their headscarfs to form a peak over their foreheads, so as to shade them from the burning sun. Sometimes a garment was so consistently worn in one position that it became fixed there. This force of habit was apparent in the costume of the Strandja women, who always wore the skirts of their upper *soukman* pinned up, originally the way of wearing them when engaged in house or field work. The original reason for this was forgotten long ago, but the habit of wearing the garment in this way had become so firmly rooted that its ornamentation – embroidery and applique work – was placed on the under part, so that it could be seen when the skirt was pinned up. The necessity of guarding the arms against

78

79

sunburn explained the presence of *narukvitsi,* arm pieces which covered the arm from wrist to elbow; they were either knitted or sewn. In many cases they became not only decorative elements but even obligatory parts of ritual costumes, for instance, those worn at weddings.

In most cases the initial dependence between work and clothing has been forgotten, but sometimes it has been given a new meaning. A distant echo of the close link between clothing and labour is the celebration of the beginning of certain farm work when suitable, but new clothes were worn for the occasion.

The variety of women's and to a considerable extent of men's costumes as worn in the towns can be explained by the close link between labour and clothing, particularly in the National Revival period. Another reason for this variety was that costumes were strongly influenced by conditions in general. The costumes worn by the women of Kotel, Panagyurishté, Koprivshtitsa, Kalofer, Karnobat, Sliven and Gabrovo, the women of the Rila region and of the town of Bansko in this period showed the same trend towards new forms of a town type, but differed in material, cut, colour, ornamentation, structure and composition because they were adapted to local working conditions.

The force of this principle made even the importance of the natural environment pale into insignificance, regardless of the population's life and work in direct contact with Nature. A comparison of the geophysical and climatic conditions in the individual

78

Girls in the festive costumes worn by *Lazarki,* taking part in the spring fertility dances on Lazarus Day in Sofia region. Early 20th century.

79

Girl from the Sofia region. Late 19th century. Painting by Ivan Mrkvička.

80

Little *Lazarki* in Sofia region. Early 20th century.

81

Girls and young men in festive costumes. Sofia region, late 19th century.

regions of the country with the spread of the basic types of costume shows no decisive dependence between clothing and the natural environment. A convincing proof of the superiority of labour over the natural environment is the use of two varieties of costumes in regions of a hilly character, not according to the seasons, but according to the cycles of activities in production. In the northern foothills of Stara Planina the two-apron costume, suitable for farm work, was worn, while the closed, comparatively warm *soukman* type was worn in a cold climate. The former was put on when the first sod was broken in spring until the last of the harvest had been gathered in; while the latter was worn chiefly in the home.

Seasonal garments are found chiefly in the southern regions of the country. The fixed points of the season are *Gyorgyovden* (St.George's Day) and *Dimitrovden* (St.Dimiter's Day), the dates in the national calendar which divide the working year into two periods, individually linked with different kinds of work in farming and stock-breeding. The seasonal garments differ in material and colour, and often in form as well.

Living so close to Nature the Bulgarians were well acquainted with the physical laws of absorption of heat by fabrics of different colours and that is why in summer, along the valley of the River Maritsa, the women wore light-coloured, smooth yellow, white or striped *sayas* or *aladjas,* as they were also called, and in winter replaced them with dark woollen *aladjas,* most often of a striped dark red and black fabric, and in more recent times, one also saw green and blue, mauve and black stripes, too. Along the valleys of the Rivers Strouma and Mesta white or blue cotton *sayas* were worn, and in winter striped woollen ones, mostly dark red and black. In the Strandja Uplands upper garments in summer were white cotton gathered skirts, while in winter a black woollen *grizh (or saya)* replaced them. The same garments were even adapted to the seasons. In the regions of Svilengrad, Harmanliy and Ivailovgrad, the women's *litaks,* another type of overdress, had sleeves that were worn in winter and taken off in summer.

The costumes of the mountain dwellers had stern straight lines which made them fit the body closely. The women's *soukmans* were made of felted woollen material and were close-fitting in the upper part, while the lower part was shaped like a trapeze, but was worn in such a way that the flares were held in at the back, so that the lower part of the body was well covered. Other examples are the white *benevretsi* (close-fitting trousers) and narrow *mentés,* jackets worn in the Western Bulgarian regions. In the Southern regions, on the other hand, we find comparatively thin cotton and unfelted woollen fabrics, made up with numerous soft folds into *soukmans.* Another illustration are the men's and women's costumes in the Stara Zagora Plain and the valley of the River Toundja.

Geographical conditions have a special influence on the structure of costumes. They are particularly rich in their basic structure with

82
Men's and women's costumes. Sofia region. Late 19th century.

83
Festive costumes worn by elderly women in Sofia region. Late 19th century.

84
Everyday costume worn by a bachelor. Sofia Region. Late 19th century. Painting by Ivan Mrkvička.

82

83

84

85

86

87

85

Bride's costume. Sofia region. Mid-19th century. Painting by Ivan Mrkvička.

86

Man's costume. Sofia region. Late 19th century.

87

Bridegroom's costume. Sofia region. Mid–19th century. Painting by Ivan Mrkvička.

a view to keeping more heat around the body. The women's costume of the Western Rhodopes is a case in point; here, a short waist-length jacket, called *saltamarka,* was constantly worn and was even artistically linked with the *soukman,* being ornamented with the same linear patterns embroidered in gold thread. The men's costumes in the mountainous regions had several upper garments as a constant part; they differed as to the cut of the sleeves and the manner of buttoning: a sleeveless bolero, an *aba* with sleeves and a *saltamarka* (short jacket) with fronts that meet or overlap. In the warm southern fields, in Haskovo and Purvomai regions, a man's outer garment was usually an *anteria, a* quilted cotton jacket; sometimes it was even made of silk, striped in two colours, the same type of fabric as was used for the women's *sayas* and *aladjas.*

There is no denying the influence of Nature, as a factor, on the artistic form of the costume, as well as on the people's mentality. The beauty of the countryside, with its characteristic variety and even contrasts – broad plains of wheat, such as those in the Dobroudja, and the Danubian Plain ; the river valleys of the Maritsa, the Toundja, the Strouma and the Mesta; fertile valleys; trim hollows, snowy peaks, among which is the Moussala, the highest in the Balkan Peninsula; dense and ancient forests, such as those of the Rhodopes; turbulent rivers, clear mountain lakes, such as those of the Rila and the Pirin Mountains; the sunny shores of the Black Sea – all these features were active in creating some of the essential features of the national character of the Bulgarians, such as their love for beauty and their constant striving to satisfy their high aesthetic demands; the efforts made to avail themselves to the maximum of all the possibilities of beautifying their environment, features whichcall to life and maintain, as they have maintained through the centuries, the varied types of decorative art that have been used in their costumes. The higher cultural level attained by the population gradually reduced the part played by the geographical environment in varying the costumes and garments worn in many regions, where natural conditions were different, and this led to a gradual disappearance of the differences.

In structure individual garments and whole costume were suitably *adapted to the physiological features* of the body. The relationship between the form of a garment and the physiological features of the body even led to bans and unwritten customary laws. The appearance of garments for various ages, and the obligatory wearing of clothes of a special cut in various cases were due to the strict observance of these relations. The little costumes worn by children possessed almost all the essential qualities required of children's clothing – softness and lightness of the weave and a cut, allowing freedom of movement.

In material and cut individual garments and whole costumes possessed the necessary *hygienic and sanitary qualities.* Almost every traditional costume can secure an artificially

88

Sleeve of woman's chemise. Sofia region. Early 20th century.

89

Embroidery on the sleeve of a woman's chemise. Sofia region. Second half of the 19th century.

88

89

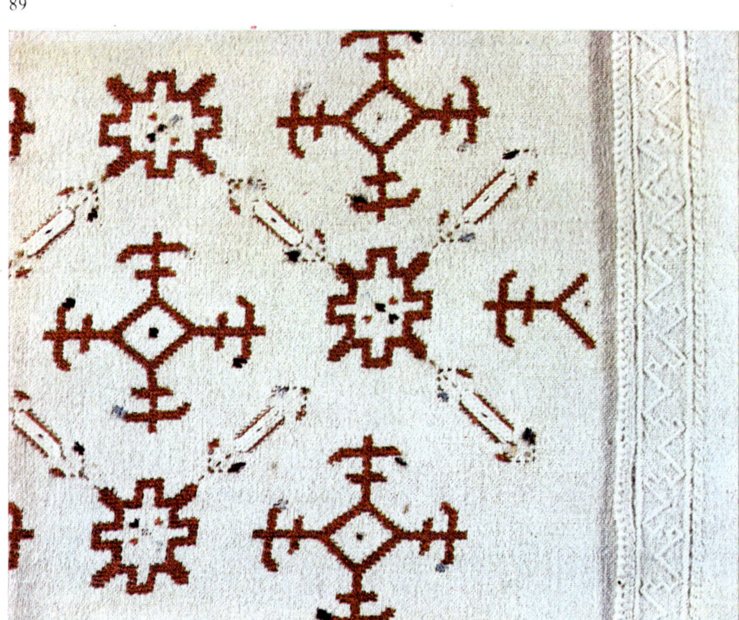

regulated climate and soften the impact of the environment.

It is apparent from the brief review of the various factors which have influenced the development of Bulgarian national costumes that they not only conditioned the creation of a variety of forms, which met the people's practical and aesthetical requirements in different parts of the country, but that they alsocontributed to the creation of local variety, thus giving an impetus to the progressive development of this essential. section of the Bulgarian people's culture, thereby increasing its variety in time and in various epochs.

Despite the great variety of their heritage; despite the different influences and borrowings; despite the many variants of basic and secondary factors and the difference in the force of their impact in various periods and different regions of the ethnic territory inhabited by the Bulgarian people, Bulgarian national costumes are united by a common composition, as well as by the decoration and the system of ist various functions.

These national costumes are intricate in composition. The complete costume, worn on holidays and ceremonial occasions, consists of a considerable number of garments and accessories, ornaments and jewellery. However, this composition is not the same in all cases, and it changes, depending on the season, labour conditions and way of life, the requirements of customs and rituals, aesthetic norms, etc. Their simplest variants are to be found when work in the fields or the household is at its height. In

90
Men's and women's belts. Sofia region, Late 19th century.

91
Embroidery on the sleeve of a woman's chemise. Sofia region. Second half of the 19th century.

90

91

92

harvest time a woman harvesting in the Danubian Plain wore only a long chemise, with one or two aprons tied on over it, one in front and one behind, instead of wearing the heavy pleated *vulnenik* or *burchnik* (skirt or kilt). But there were no costumes consisting of only one garment.

92
Embroidery on the sleeve of a woman's chemise. Sofia region. Mid-19th century.

The chemise was the foundation garment in all costumes. In form and material it was one of the most essential uniting elements in Bulgarian costumes it was made of hemp, linen, and in more recent times of cotton or silk fabrics; it was long, made with sleeves and ornamented with textiles. The function of the chemise in the various stages of development of national clothing was common to costumes in the country. In old costumes, for instance in the men's summer working clothes, worn in the Danubian Plain and the Pirin region, or in the women's costumes for house and field work in Northern Bulgaria and the Rhodopes, which consisted of a long chemise, bound only with a waistband or an apron, the chemise was at one and the same time an under and an upper garment. In the traditional form of the regular costumes only certain parts of the chemise played this double part – in the one– and two-apron costume only the upper part and lower edge of the chemise's skirts played these parts, while in the *soukman* costume, only the breast part, the sleeves and skirts were visible and in the *saya* costume, only the skirts , and in certain variants, also the lower half of the sleeves. The same thing is seen in the men's costumes – the upper part of the shirt was the only garment in

93
Embroidery on the sleeve of a woman's chemise. Sofia region. Second half of the 19th century.

93

94

94
Embroidery on the sleeve of a woman's chemise. Sofia region. Mid-19th century.

the man's costumes worn with *benevretsi* or *potouri,* while in the later costumes in which sleeveless upper garments were worn, only parts of the shirt were visible. In more recent times the shirt has become an entirely under garment, completely covered by long upper garments with sleeves. The women's costumes of the Central Rhodopes are a typical example of this: the *soukman* has acquired long sleeves and the skirts have become considerably longer. In the men's black garment costumes the shirt was entirely covered by long-sleeved upper garments. The separate skirts sewn onto the edges of the *soukman* or the *saya* of a woman's costume are reminiscent of the chemise's function as an upper garment.

The aspect of a costume is usually defined by its upper garments. In the old costumes, the upper garments were still assisted by the chemise or other parts, as those which gave them their form; however, they gradually undertook this role themselves. This process was preceded by a transition of the garments to more advanced forms. The black skirt, made from one width of fabric, gradually took on the form of a closed garment and covered almost whole of the lower part of the chemise, while its upper part was covered by a special upper garment. As a repetition of the chemise, the *soukman* at first covered only its principal parts, but

95

Embroidery on the sleeve of a woman's chemise. Pernik region. Mid-19th century.

96

Embroidery on the sleeve of a woman's chemise. Pernik region. Mid-19th century.

95

96

it gradually took on the shape of a long garment with or without sleeves. The *saya* also changed its development: from an outer movable garment of unstable components, it became a long garment with sleeves, which took on the purpose of giving its complete aspect to the costume. In the men's costumes worn of old the sleeves of the shirt were usually allowed to show white, while the silhouette was outlined by upper garments, wide open down the front and flared at the bottom. In the more recent black-garment costumes upper garments with long sleeves, closed down the front, formed their typical appearance. Similar examples indicate a common principle in upper and under garments, forming parts of a costume, but developing at different rates in different epochs.

The waistband appeared as the key element of the costume; it was wound around the waist over all the garments which formed the basic elements of the costumes. Certain local costumes emphasize this role. For instance, the men's costume of the Sofia region with its waistband wound directly over the shirt shows its initial place there with the shirt as the only upper and under garment of a man's costume. As the basic composition of the costumes increased, the waistband was worn over certain upper garments, too. The costumes of Graovo and Znepolé are proof of

97 98

Embroidery around the hem of a woman's chemise. Trun region. Second half of the 19th century.

97

98

99

100

99
Man's costume. Trun region. Late 19th century. Painting by Ivan Mrkvička.

100
Young men's *horo*. Bourgas region. Early 20th century.

this: the waistband was wound here at end of the short white jacket. In Bulgarian national costumes the waistband plays the part of a uniting element in fabric, form,dimensions and ornament. It varies from a knitted tie to a wide thick woven waistband long enough to be wound several times around the waist, ornamented with bright colours and patterns woven into the fabric.

The essential element which united the women's costume was the apron. It is absent in only a few local costumes, such as those of the Western Sofia Region, in Znepolé, Graovo, Karlovo and Plovdiv regions. Many local costumes show that it gradually changed from a purely utilitarian garment to one of the most vividly decorative focuses of the costume with the rich variety of its fabrics and ornamentation.

The old outer garments were a uniting element in the costumes of both sexes. They were made of woolen fabrics, most often white, open down the front, below the waist in length or reaching down to the knees, with flared skirts, sleeveless or with long or short sleeves. The more recent variants of these garments changed in colour, dimensions and cut, but continued to maintain their link with the old forms. However, while these garments gradually became an inseparable part of the basic composition of the men's costumes, they were used chiefly as parts of the women's costumes on festive or ritual occasions. Their use was established by the strict rules of customs and rituals and served chiefly to indicate family status.

101

102

101

Everyday woman's costume from Pomorie region.

102

Girls in festive costumes. Pomorie region. Early 20th century.

Besides these parts of the costumes, an important part was played in their general aspect by accessories, ornaments, and a variety of hair-dos and the manner in which the head scarf was worn.

A wreath, a *kossichnik* (ornament attached to the back of the head and hanging down over the hair) and a nosegay were common elements in a girl's complex hair-do, formed by a large number of tiny plaits gathered in one common pigtail down the back or left hanging free, but joined together in such a way as never to let them fall over the shoulder, or get in the way of the girl's work; coins and flowers were woven into the plaits by way of decoration.

A bride's white head scarf indicated her status in the family as a married woman. One of its principal purposes, according to the unwritten laws of folk customs, was to cover the hair completely and keep it out of sight. Men wore their hair long at the back and tousled, with a forelock, and also covered. The picture of a Bulgarian is not to be thought of without a fur hat, although it varied in shape – semi-cylindrical, shaped like a mushroom, as worn in certain villages of Sofia region, and around Pomorié; cylindrical, as in the Stara Planina Mountains, the Sredna Gora and Thrace; coneshaped, as in the Dobroudja. Men did not take off their *kalpaks,* as these hats were called, either at work in the fields or the workshop, when visiting, at weddings and merrymakings. Certain data indicate that at one time hats were made of felted

103

104

105

material, but they disappeared comparatively early, being only retained somewhat longer in the Rhodopes, among the shepherds. An underhat of red cloth was also worn with a fur hat or independently, and preserved until late in the Sofia region and North-Western Bulgaria.

The boat-shaped sandals with a blunt or pointed tip, made of pig- or ox-skin, were also generally worn. Blunt-tipped sandals predominated in the Western regions of the country, and the *vruvchanki,* which had a dense network of laces across the front, was another variety. Sandals with pointed tips were worn in the Eastern regions. *Navoushta,* pieces of cloth, wrapped around the leg and held in place by lacings, were worn by men and women alike. But while they continued to be worn by men quite late, women exchanged them for stockings fairly early, which they knitted themselves in multi-coloured wools; or they wore *kaltsouni,* also made of cloth, which covered the leg from knee to ankle; or *laktouni,* which came up over the ankle, or *tarlitsi,* which only covered the foot.

Accessories were also worn with Bulgarian national costumes which, besides their use and decorative function, also indicated the wearer's position in his social environment. Men and women wore handkerchiefs with richly decorated corners tucked into their belts or waistbands; aside from their practical use, they added a festive touch to the costume. At the same time, the way they were worn and their number indicated the wearer's position in the family.

103 104

Grandfather and grandson shepherds from Pomorié region. Early 20th century.

105

Apron from Pomorié region. Early 20th century.

106

107

108

106
Festive girl's costume. Varna region. Late 19th century.

107
Koledar (carol singer). Varna region. Late 19th century.

108
Koledari. Varna region Early 20th century.

Another typical feature in the composition of the Bulgarian national costume was the harmonious combination of its individual parts. The wearers of these costumes were able to satisfy their own taste and their sense of beauty in putting them together, since they made most of the fabrics and fashioned them themselves. Each part of the costume was a work of art in itself; it was worn for practical purposes, but the harmony and beauty of the whole costume were never lost sight of. Each part had its well-defined place and relationship to the other parts. Some were essential to the costume, other parts were subordinated to them; others again were decorative, as well as constructive elements, while yet others completed the outline of the silhouette. However, for practical purposes, the parts and the whole formed an artistic unit.

109

110

111

112

113

114

115

109

Man's and woman's costumes. Shoumen region. Late 19th century.

110

Embroidery around the hem of a woman's chemise. Provadiya region. Late 19th century.

111

Embroidery on the ends of head scarves of the *messal* Type. Provadiya region. Late 19th century.

112

Young woman's festive costume. Silistra region. Second half of the 19th century.

113

Young bride's costume. Toutrakan region. Late 19th century.

114

Aprons from Toutrakan region. Early 20th century.

115

Man's and woman's costumes. Silistra region. Early 20th century.

ARTISTIC ARRANGEMENT

Strivings to achieve beauty and a closer contact with it, to attain its heights, and realize the aesthetic ideal of a personality harmoniously developed in every way; to build up a more perfect society – all these strivings formed one of the principal impulses which urged people to turn their costumes into works of art. Setting aside the Bulgarian people's attitude to beauty,from the point of view of pure consumption, these costumes show the people themselves to have been their creators. Most of the traditional costumes can be considered as the fruit of inspiration, taken as a whole and in their individual parts.

Bulgarian women always looked upon the creation of the family's clothes as inspired creative labour. It must not be forgotten that they produced the fabrics, fashioned them, composed the costumes and decorated them. In this long process they were guided by their sense of beauty, which gave life even to inanimate objects. In making garments it is not enough to have mastered to perfection the technology of weaving, cutting, embroidering, knitting and sewing – they all have to be used with love. Old women remember the sleepless nights of creative restlessness and joy at seeing their visions take shape, and their absorbtion was so total that they thought of nothing but the work at hand; how to get exactly the colours they wanted from the natural dyes they used; how to design a better pattern for their embroidery, and how to put together the parts of the costume to obtain the best effect. Experienced old embroideresses in the Balkan Range, the Valley of Roses and the Valley of the River Strouma tell us that in their youth they were mistresses of their craft to the same extent as the literate were masters of letters: 'Just as you write letters, so we embroider stitches,' or 'what writing is to you, embroidery is to us,' they would say, and they did not mean simply to explain their

116

117

skill in the technology of embroidery, but also the part it played as a means of expressing creative emotions, a world outlook, an attitude to the community, etc. For them it was what words are for poets and writers.

The idea of a beautiful costume as the final result of her work inspired the Bulgarian woman. She embroidered with 'a merry heart', and the rhythm of her actions was accompanied by her own singing: 'Fine stitches she stitched', A song she sang', 'Her heart was merry' (Smolyan). A more suitable definition of the exciting impact of creative labour can hardly be found than that of the folksinger, according to whom the inspired work of production affected even inanimate objects. While she was weaving her fabric 'the blocks were singing a song.'

The idea of a 'beautiful costume' filled every moment of the long process of preparing it. It began with collecting the raw material for the fabric, passed through the processing, delayed long over the structure and modelling of the garments, composing the whole costume and ornamenting it. The selection of the textile materials according to quality was done with a view to the practical and utilitarian use to which the fabrics made of them were to be put. Thus wool, linen, hemp, and silk of several qualities were set aside for the purpose. The materials were processed also according to the use to which they were to be put, being spun or twisted to certain requirements. Different weaving techniques were used to obtain different grades of fabric in thickness, design and ornamentation, and to this end different instuments were used, although at first sight the differences in them were slight. In such cases the weavers appeared not only as experienced technologists, but also as constructors of mechanical and technical devices, always with a view to achieving an artistic result. Bulgarian women deserve

116

Bachelors in festive garb. Silistra region. Early 20th century.

117

Children from Silistra region. Early 20th century.

118

119

118

Apron from Silistra region, Early 20th century.

119

Apron from Silistra region, Late 19th century.

high praise for their work in the past, particularly when the unfavourable conditions under which they worked are borne in mind. Her workshop was usually a room with a low ceiling, lit by a small window, even by the opening of the chimney, the light of the fire on the hearth, apiece of burning pinewood or an oil lamp. In the spring she moved her work out to the wattle fence, where the girls would gather in the sunshine, vying with one another in embroidering their spring costumes; or in autumn at the work parties along the roads; or in the summer *belenki* (bleaching parties) along the river banks or at fountains or wells. The degree to which inspired creative work went into the artistic formation of the costumes is shown by the manner in which the primitive instruments they used were decorated. Thus, distaffs and spindles were 'written', i.e. ornamented with flat carving; the fabrics were prepared on a 'gilded loom'; the embroidery was stitched with 'a little silver needle' and with 'gilded threads' and on a 'bone frame'; the fabrics were bleached with a 'gilded beetle'. A poetic touch was also given to the constant maintenance of the costumes: they were washed in 'the White Danube', beetled on a 'marble stone', dried on a rose bush, folded on a carnation so that they would look like roses.

The implements they used were most often a wooden domestic loom, and in some regions even in the not so remote past, its supports were dug into the earthen floor (in the Vratsa and Mihailovgrad districts); wooden distaffs and spindles, even the primitive instrument, called *mahalka,* adapted to drawing threads out of flax, hemp, cotton and silk, wool and goatshair, a metal needle and a wooden hook were used. The Bulgarian decorative artist had also made a device for herself which played the part of a palette – a wooden *koprinarka,* a silk spool in the form of a spindle, grooved along its length, on which silk threads of various colours were wound, by means of which she formed her colour combinations.

As a dressmaker, the Bulgarian woman in the past had her own measurements, she most often used parts of the body as a measure: *lakut* – elbow, *pedya,* and *cheperek* span, *krachka,* step, foot, but she managed to make clothes which fitted the body with them. The basic garments were usually made of whole pieces of fabric in their natural width, and the necessary length. For instance, the basic part of a tunic-shaped garment like the chemise, a *soukman,* etc., was a piece of cloth of double length from shoulder toknee or ankle, folded in two, one half forming the back and the other the front. Width at the sides was obtained by adding a rectangle of a whole piece of fabric, or trapeze-shaped parts shaped from whole lengths. Chemises of the *burchanka* type also had two separate lengths of fabric according to the height of the personwhowouldwear them, joined at the shoulders by the tips of the upper edges which had been previously gathered or pleated. The sleeves were also made of whole pieces of fabric, one, one and a half, or two lengths. The collar was made of a straight piece, etc. Even separate connected elements were most often formed of parts of whole lengths of fabric, half, a quarter or an eighth of the width of the fabric. This manner of cutting ensured a maximum saving of material. Usually no fabric was left unused on the work tables of the cutters and dressmakers. However, intricate cuts were also to be found in traditional Bulgarian garments, usually chiefly in outer garments. The various decorated seams and hems, which became embroideries and laces, show how they were turned into decorative elements.

The inconveniences of the places where work was done and the

120

Young woman's festive costume. Silistra region. Mid-20th century.

121

Head scarf and jewellery as worn by a young woman. Silistra region, Mid20th-century.

120

121

primitive nature of the implements used were chiefly compensated for by a wide range of knowledge, their skilful use and mastery of the crafts involved, all motivated by the great sense of beauty and the vitality of the people.

The creative impulse, which went into the fashioning of garments is one of the essential traits in the national character of the Bulgarians; it also showed their poetic perception of their environment, their vivid imagination, a subtle taste and a perpetual striving for beauty, which all went into the creation of their costumes.

This artistic sense was one of the finest qualities possessed by Bulgarian women. Although they were worn while working and were made with a view to hygiene these costumes never lost their artistic value, nor the fine sense which went into composing and ornamenting them.

Turning material benefits, such as clothing, into works of art was not the result of vanity, but was due to aesthetic principles. The lasting value and vitality of aesthetics in the clothing of the Bulgarians can be explained by their idea of the beauty of man, and particularly of woman. In quality, this clothing had to correspond to the physical and moral virtues of the Bulgarian woman who, according to the folk-singer, was usually 'as tall and slender as a poplar', 'as white and red as an apple', or 'a bunch of roses', with a gait in which she 'swayed like a cypress, and bent like a reed', with eyes like 'two black cherries', eyebrows like 'sea leeches', and 'hair like a plaited braid'. But the ideal physical image had to be combined with virtues as far as work and social relations went. Besides being 'as lovely as could be', a girl should also be 'good at work.'

The ideal image of a man, who aroused admiration with his

122
Elderly woman's costume. Mihailovgrad region. Late 19th century.

123
Ornament on front opening of a *soukman*. Mihailovgrad region. Late 19th century.

124
Girl's festive costume. Mihailovgrad region. Mid-19th century.

122

123

124

125

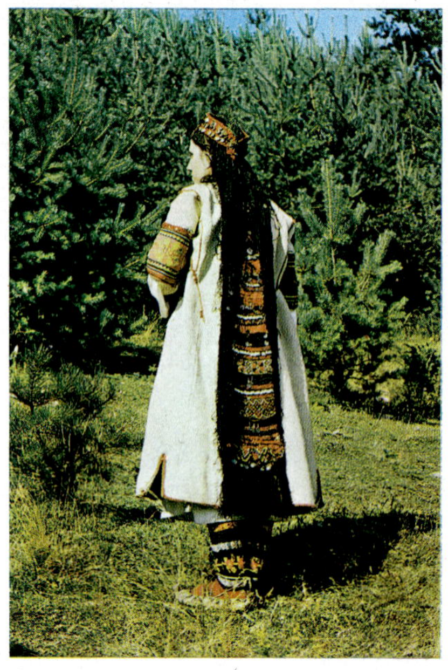

126

127

perfection, and even amazement and wonder whether he was the creation of skilled craftsmen, who had 'wrought him out of gold' or 'cast him out of silver', to whom even an unearthly origin was attributed – that 'he was taken from the sun' – this ideal image inspired Bulgarian women to create costumes of unique beauty for him, intended to satisfy the aesthetic requirements of the Bulgarians for the harmonious development of a physical and a spiritual personality.

The height of artistic skill made of garments the most cherished desires of the young people.

Beautiful clothing figured in the last wishes of Bulgarians. Old men and women always asked to be buried in their wedding garb, because they were usually 'the most beautiful'. A fine appearance was also the last wish of revolutionaries, who were sacrificing their life for national freedom and social justice, and who wanted to be well dressed, 'to have a white shirt, to have his forelock combed, and his boots shining glossily.'

Bulgarian women used various forms of decorative art in fashioning her family's clothing, but it should be noted that there was never any overornamentation or exaggeration in the costumes they made. Moderation and discretion, and forms only lightly hinted at predominated in their work. The sheen of metal thread, large areas in one bright colour were rarely to be found; only moderate brilliance was required of the ornaments woven into the structure of the costumes, the soft, subdued sheen which appeared when light fell on their exquisite and small details.

However, the beauty of the costumes was attained mainly through textile decoration – fabric, embroidery, knitting and crochet work, appliqué work in part, and edgings. Even though all these were obtained from use of a variety of techniques the

125
Festive winter costume (front view) of a young bride. Mihailovgrad region. Mid-19th century.

126
Festive winter costume (back view) of a young bride. Mihailovgrad region. Mid-19th century

127
Costume worn by an elderly shepherd in Mihailovgrad region. Late 19th century.

128

129

130

128
Girl in summer costume. Vratsa region Painting by Ivan Mrkvička. Late 19th century.

129
Girl in winter costume. Vratsa region. Late 19th century.

130
Costume worn by an elderly man. Oryahovo region. Late 19th century. Painting by Ivan Mrkvička.

branches of textile ornamentation were united by their artistry. Bulgarian decorative fabrics, embroideries and knitting and crochet work have a wide range of themes. The motifs, basic as well as supplementary, were inspired by what the women who made them saw around them. Predominant motifs are eloquent of their striving toachieve unity between art, life and Nature, and to to show in the idiom of ornamentation their wish to draw near to the beautiful and vital world around them. Geometrical fiqures, from simplest to the most intricate in various combinations are to be found in the patterns, but rhomboids were the most frequently met with, followed by triangles, polygonal figures and star shapes. These ornaments, and particularly their names, show that Bulgarian weavers, embroideresses and knitters transferred practically the whole of the plant and animal world around them to their handiwork. Flowers from their gardens, meadows and forest glades, fruit-trees and vines, fruits and seeds, parts and the whole body of domestic fowls and animals, and more rarely of insects, wild animals: cocks, ducks, the leg or wing of a sparrow, a pigeon, the footstep of a cat, ants, a hamster, a silkworm, a bear's foot, the tracks of a rabbit, and in more recent times the whole figures of horses and lions can be found in their work. Human figures are not depicted independently and as an aim in themselves, but most often in groups, for instance, in a chain dance, in a horseback procession. Implements of labour and household utensils are also depicted in fabrics for garments, such as ploughs, goads , a tailor's scissors, scrapers, candlesticks and pots.

These patterns had geometrical outlines, chiefly because this made them easier to work. The patterns in fabrics, embroideries and knitting were based on the number of threads and stitches, and for that reason the outlines were formed of straight lines, broken up. Thus, for instance, the disc of the sun became a rhomboid; the rosette of a flower – a polygon, an ant – a small straight line, a scraper – a triangle, scissors – an X-shaped figure. These images were reduced to an extreme degree in order to make them proportional to the surface on which they were placed: a collar, a breast piece, the edges of sleeves and skirts. Thus, a human figure became a collection of a triangle for the head, a rectangle for the body and lines for the limbs; a bird was formed by a small rectangle for the head, straight lines for the neck and a rectangle for the body. Always with a view to the place which they were to occupy, the ornaments were small. The images of even the largest animals took up only a few centimetres; pine-trees, oaks and elms were only one, two or three centimetres high. Even the smallest flowers were not shown in their natural dimensions on the fabric, embroidery or knitting pattern.

In spite of the conventions which governed the technical fulfilment and the accepted restrictions of position, Bulgarian women, who were principally responsible for the textile ornamentation of clothing, succeeded in transmitting the characteristic features of the object depicted – the forms and colours of flowers, trees and fruit, the silhouettes of animals and people, and even their expressions and moods. This was achieved by means of the supple finely broken-up contour, a drawing, which was generally true to life, and which included the most essential features of a definite subject and particularly the colouring. The breaking up of the figures, the detailed presentation of each element in them, were characteristic features of textile ornaments, and this gave them looseness, almost to the extent of openwork, and great finesse. They usually stood out vividly against the background of the fabric with their delicately drawn and coloured outlines. They

131
Embroidery on the sleeve of a woman's chemise. Vratsa region. Late 19th century.

132
Bruchnik (back skirt). Vratsa region. Second half of the 19th century.

131

132

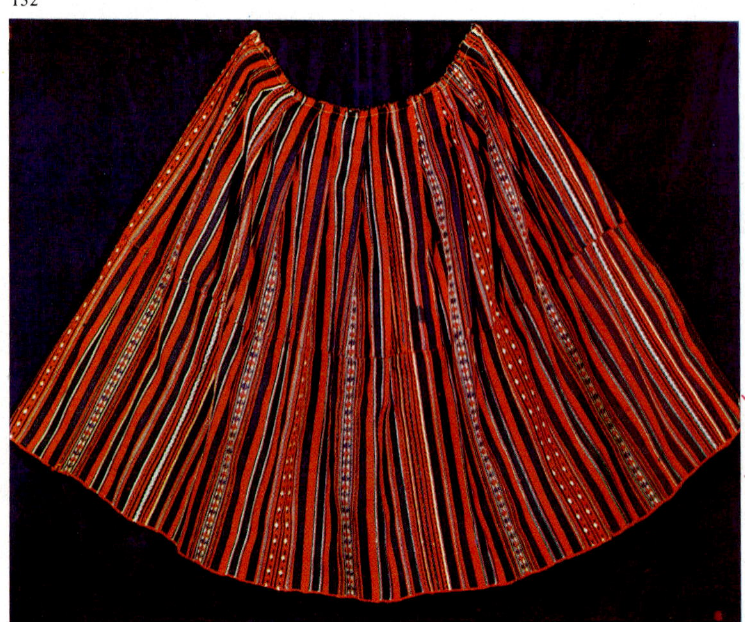

were mainly to be found in the embroideries of the Sofia district, Graovo and Znepolé, and the negatively outlined ornaments, in which the outlines were formed by the white background of the fabric, the inside being filled in with stitchery.

Colour played the most important part in indicating what the ornaments were meant to be. A figure with vague outlines was chiefly explained by the suitable distribution of the spots of colour. In Bulgarian textile ornamentation the gamut of colour was not very rich, but a great variety of shades in one colour was a characteristic feature. Each colour appeared in a countless range of tones and nuances which created an impression of many colours. Red, the colour most frequently used on fabrics, embroideries and knitting, was found in numerous tones, from the lightest delicate rose to the darkest crimson. The dyes, most often obtained from roots, barks, leaves, blossoms, seeds and the fruit of plants of the Bulgarian flora, seem tobring to the fabrics, embroideries and knitwear all the variety of colour in Bulgarian fields, and the dark soft tones of forest glades. The various colours merge in harmonies and softly shaded combinations, or strong and daring contrasts; but they are always pleasant and fine. Colours were used as a constructive element not only in separate ornaments, but also in whole compositions. A design in which patterns of the same outlines alternated rhythmically was often to be met with.

For its part rhythm is one of the elements of the composition which created the beauty of Bulgarian embroideries, fabrics and knitwear to a great extent. Motifs of the same form but in different colours were usually placed in rows, in a calm and smooth, or a lively and playful rhythm, or two different motifs alternated. In some compositions there would be a central motif, surrounded

133
Man's winter costume. Vratsa region. Second half of the 19th century.

134
Bachelor's everyday costume. Belogradchik region. Late 19th century. Painting by Ivan Mrkvička.

135
Man's winter costume from Belogradchik region. Late 19th century.

133

134

135

136

137

138

by other, smaller ones as, for instance, in the fabrics of aprons in the Sliven, Yambol, Lovech and Dobroudja regions. Other motifs were found in larger dimensions and combined with more numerous details. Outstanding examples in this respect were to be found in the Samokov and Stankedimitrov regions, where embroideries along the lower half of the sleeves of the chemise look like branches of blossom, bent under the weight of open and budding blossoms, around which wreaths of leaves seem to have been blown by a spring breeze.

The wonderful artistic achievements of Bulgarian textile ornamentation is largely due to a skilful choice of material and a variety of techniques. The relief, soft tones of the fabrics, embroideries and knitwear were achieved by the use mainly of woollen yarns, the smooth texture and sheen of the fabric and the brilliance of the silks used for embroidery. In more recent times cotton threads were also used. Several techniques of weaving and embroidery were used on one and the same motif. A grain-like surface in embroidery was obtained by the use of cross stitch; smoothness – by half-stitch, a straight or split stitch; their slight relief was obtained by knots, and their transparency by open work – all these stitches used in several variants. However, whatever stitches and techniques were used, artistic requirements were never lost sight of.

The technology of all varieties of textile ornamentation were known all over the country, but in the Western regions embroidery was chiefly used to ornament garments, while in the Eastern regions, the weave was the chief element. Knitting, crocheting and needle-point lace were also used and reached great artistic levels in the Western regions.

Needle-point lace was much more rarely used on Bulgarian folk

136

Man's spring costume from Belogradchik region. Late 19th century.

137

Bachelors' costumes. Belogradchik region. Late 19th century.

138

Children in festive costumes from Belogradchik region. Late 19th century.

139
Children dancing. Belogradchik region. Late 19th century.

140
Grandfather and grandson on the way to the field. Belogradchik region. Late 19th century

141
Shepherd from Belogradchik region. Late 19th century.

costumes by way of decoration, but it had great artistic qualities. This lace was usually unnoticed at first sight, but its airy designs lent both garments and accessories ornamented with it particular delicacy. These designs were transparent and formed a contrast with the comparatively thicker and even rough handwoven fabrics of which the garments were made, and therefore softened their stern outlines and stiff folds.

Needle-point lace was usually worked along seams, and stood out above edges, but chiefly on parts of the garment which were visible. This lace obviously appeared as a result of the artistic demands made on clothing. They were usually beautifully worked and made the seams decorative elements. The variety of stitches used on the garments which formed the men's and women's costumes in various parts of the country marked the different stages in their artistic composition. The finest development and finish was noted in the 'nets' and 'loops' on the sleeves and skirts of women's chemises in the regions of Kotel, Preslav, Sliven, Yambol, Ivailovgrad, Razlog, Gotsedelchev and Smolyan; on the 'spiders' worked on aprons in the regions of Pomorié, Silistra, Sliven and Yambol, and between the multicoloured strips of fabric appliquéd on the skirts of the *soukmans* in the regions of Karnobat, Provadiya, Shoumen, Sliven, Yambol and Groudovo. The needle lace worked in white silk on the skirts of chemises almost merged into the fabric, and it was only their openwork quality which betrayed their presence and their decorative role. Their value was also enhanced by colour – some local varieties were worked in yellow silk. The 'spiders' worked in coloured yarns on the aprons in Thrace became a type of embroidery.

This finely stitched needle-point lace has made such a place for itself in folk aesthetics and became so customary that even when

142

143

144

it was not necessary to join seams, it was used as a fabric or embroidery, like the 'spiders' on the aprons of Sliven, Yambol and Karnobat regions. These artistically worked seams also led to the appearance of lace with its own independent ornamentation which could be used everywhere. On the aprons of Tolbukhin, Varna and Pomorié regions they were independent works of artistic crochet work and needle-point.

Bulgarian women have also achieved a great deal in working needle-point lace along the edges of garments and head scarves. While as a general rule needle-point lace was used to ornament traditional costumes, the type worked as edgings were mainly linked with the costumes worn in towns in the National Revival period. The type, known as *kenéta,* was very popular in certain towns and villages of the Sredna Gora region, and later in other centres, such as Plovdiv and Assenovgrad. This type of lace was particularly beautiful made by the deft fingers of the Koprivshtitsa women at the turn of the 19th and 20th centuries. They were inevitable elements of the festive costume of an urban type. Sewn to the edges of the chemise opening at the neckline, and the edges of its long sleeves, the delicate white or coloured lace was usually the only decoration of the costume, made of Eastern silks and velvet, or even from fine handwoven dark woollen material. The needlewomen of Koprivshtitsa laboured for hours at their needle-point lace and reproduced on it the flowers of their gardens and the fields, songbirds of the forest, and architectural details, such as the arched bridges of their birthplace, even human figures, not in solitary splendour, but as a genre scene, usually a chain dance. The lace was several centimetres wide as a rule and in it blossomed hollyhocks, columbines, pansies, snowdrops, little roses, whole pots of flowers and little peppers; while cocks

142

Young woman in everyday winter costume. Belogradchik region. Late 19th century.

143

Old woman in winter costume. Belogradchik region. Late 19th century.

144

Embroidery on the front opening of a man's chemise. Belogradchik region. Late 19th century.

145

145

Young men's and women s *horo*. Vidin region. Late 19th century.

crowed, a cock's comb stood out, 'eyes' stared at you from them, and a chain dance of 'dollies' was there to delight you.

Despite the possibility of naturalistic imagery, the women who sewed this lovely lace showed themselves to be real decorative artists and used almost the same principles of stylization as were used in fabrics and embroidery. The techniques used made it possible to achieve delicate treatment, and open-work space, as well as a rounded and supple design. The little figures were reduced in size and synthesized in so far as the laws of decorative art required this, so that the original images should not lose their essence and even their vitality, while at the same time giving a marked artistic effect. Colours also helped to make the image created resemble the object it was intended to represent – a delicate mauve shade seemed to breathe the scent of forest violets, pink reminded one of roses, white – of snowdrops, and so on.

Needle-point lace together with crocheted lace gradually displaced embroidery as decoration for garments, more so in the towns than in the villages, while crocheted lace took a firm hold in the villages. Brightly coloured *sarafluks* (types of needle-point lace) and *sachaks* (another name for this lace) became the most popular ornamentation for head scarves. *Bademi,* most often composed of multi-coloured triangular figurines, completed certain garments, such for instance, as the aprons of the Smolyan region. Bulgarian women were familiar with applique work, usually used when brilliant spots of colour were required.

It should be emphasized that applique work was not used in practically any region of the country as the sole and principal manner of ornamenting a garment. It was usually combined with a decorative fabric, embroidery, edgings, etc. In all these cases the

146

147

146

Young woman's everyday summer costume. Vidin region. Late 19th century

147

Woman's *burchanka* chemise. Vidin region. Second half of the 19th century

patch appliqued was not an independent and completely finished ornament of the garment, but a basis for new decoration intended to introduce more colour against the background of the dark fabric of the garment. For instance, strips called *belki,* were usually placed on the skirts of *soukmans;* they were pieces of cloth and dyed cocoons, tapes, small coins and paillettes, and were also surrounded by embroidery. The stictly geometrical outlines of these strips in the regions of Sliven, Kotel, Yambol, Karnobat and Aitos were softened by the elongated stitches of the seams worked with yellow silk between the strips, in such a way as to be almost like lace on the multi-coloured strips embroidered above them. This supplementary appliqué work did more than reduce the unicoloured areas of the strips, introducing colour and figures in the design and giving it more relief, relieving the monotony of their forms and sizes. Through these additional decorations, the appliquéd strips harmonized with the style of Bulgarian textile ornamentation, the distinctive features of which were careful details, a supple design and a rich gamut of colour.

Appliqué work was one of the marked signs of a knowledge and the use of the 'idiom of colours'. The varied colour combinations indicated age, family status and the state of the persons who wore the clothes.

The bright colours of appliquéd strips were considered the privilege of the young, particularly young brides. Old and elderly women wore *soukmans* without strips, or only embroidered.

Appliqué work on outer garments was more markedly decorative in character, particularly on the white outer garments of Northern and Western Bulgaria and other regions of the country. Patches of red cloth and strips which followed the seams along the back, the tips of the inset flares, or fronts with a great variety of edges:

148

149

148
Girl s everyday summer costume. Vidin region. Painting by Ivan Mrkvička. Second half of the 19th century.

149
Embroidery on the sleeve of a woman's chemise. Vidin region. Second half of the 19th century.

straight, indented, festooned, etc., were the most frequent ornamentation on the short jackets worn by women. However, the use of appliquéd strips and patches showed a striving to complete the structure of the costume, not only to introduce patterns and colour into the smooth white or dark surfaces of the garments. In this case, this type of ornamentation was not an end in itself, nor even only a way of ornamenting it; it played a constructive role in the whole artistic design of the costume.

In other cases when appliqué work was used on Bulgarian garments, which formed part of a costume, the relief it supplied and the bright colours of the patches were used with great artistry. Large plant ornaments, embroidered by counting the threads of the fabric, were met with on the skirts of the *soukmans* of Kazanluk and Yambol regions; they were supplemented with small squares of cloth, not larger than half a centimetre a side, sewn around them. These small patches were usually sewn onto empty spaces in the pattern and completed it. At the same time they enhanced the embroidery with their bright red colour.

Appliquéd patches formed the most frequent ornamentation of sheepskin jackets and other leather work. Embroideries were not typical as a form of working leather and sheepskin jackets in Bulgaria. Red, green and blue pieces of leather of different shapes and sizes were sewn onto the front of women's and also men's sheepskin jackets. These patches stood out particularly well on the white background of the smooth leather. Even the figures of men were sometimes used in this type of ornamentation.

Another form of leather ornamentation was appliquéing plaits along the edges and skirts of these jackets, and even of separate little strips, sometimes formed into spirals, concentric circles, etc. *Braiding* was one of the extensively used ornamentations in

150

151

152

Bulgarian costumes all over the country. At first the use of braid was a practical device to keep the seams from splitting. The braid, inserted between the two pieces of cloth being sewn together, strengthened the seams and kept them in shape. In such places braid had a decorative purpose as well. The white strings along the ends and seams of the thick *yamourlouks* (shepherds' capes), made of dark homespun, outlined their shapes, and made their structure more harmonious. The black edgings on the light-coloured tufted blankets and *yamourlouks* in light colours played the same part, and were enriched by new elements which made them more artistic. In part they were sewn onto the fabric in a variety of patterns, or they became lace-like and were worked along the edge of the garment, forming a frame for it. Ornamentation in the form of linear patterns belonged to the first group, and it was worked on the garments and along the seams, while the braiding on women's *soukmans* and *sayas* belonged to the second group.

A variety of ornamentation made of fabrics was to be found on Bulgarian folk clothing, and some of them were most impressive and aristic.

These decorations on the costumes in their varied forms – fabrics, embroideries, knitting edgings and appliqué work, had a close link with the articles they were worked on, and combinations of their forms in common. They not only gave character to whole costumes, but in design and colour were even adapted to the individual parts of these costume. For instance, on one and the same garment the embroideries on the collar, around the front opening, the sleeves and the skirts coincided in content, composition and even in colour scheme. The embroidery on the collar was usually an uninterrupted row of motifs; along the sleeve edges, it

150
Embroidery on the sleeve of a woman's chemise. Vidin region. Second half of the 19th century.

151
Vulnenik (back skirt). Vidin region. Second half of the 19th century.

152
Embroidery on the front of a man's shirt. Vidin region. Late 19th century.

153

154

153 154
Festive women's summer costumes worn by *Banat Bulgarians.* Vratsa region. Early 20th century.

was, as a rule, a perpendicularly placed row of elements, going down the whole length of the sleeve and even merging into a common area, forming chains of elements or linked with one another; on the skirts there was usually a garland of ornaments. All decorative elements were placed in suitable positions, which give added beauty to the garment. They formed part of a whole. Thus, for instance, the parts of the men's and women's costumes of the Sofia region were united by white spirals and hooks on the dark blue or black cloth of the *soukman* or the man's *menté* (short jacket); the costumes of the Strandja Uplands – by the flame-red embroidery and weaving on shirts, chemises, aprons and stockings; the costumes of Yambol region – by the multi-coloured, cheerful and lively outlines of the ornaments on the weave of the aprons and the embroideries on *soukmans* and chemises; those of the Rila region – by the delicate outlines and multi-coloured plant ornaments on the clothes; the costumes of Roussé district – by the large and thickly embroidered motifs in a brilliant orange on the chemise and the pleated skirt.

A characteristic feature of textile ornamentation among Bulgarians should be noted here – its intricacy and numerous combinations. Almost none of the various kinds of textile ornaments was used independently in the complete artistic form of the garment or object. The decorative weave was combined with edgings, embroidery and more rarely with appliqué work; embroidery, for its part, was combined with the fabric, appliqué work and crocheting or needle-point; crocheting and needle-point were combined with embroidery. They were linked not only to enhance the complete decoration of the articles, but also to intensify the effect of each of them and to facilitate the work of ornamentation. Thus, for instance, a decorative fabric was enhanced by embroidery, in working small multi-coloured elements which it was difficult to achieve on a loom. Whole surfaces of fabrics, as is the case with the belts woven in Sofia district, were covered with embroidery, so as to vary the ornamentation and introduce a greater variety of colour. The stockings knitted in the Sofia, Samokov and Pernik regions have patterns knitted onto them, but the patterns on the front were also outlined with embroidery, and new motifs were worked on them to give the whole ornament greater relief. The various kinds of combinations between fabric ornamentation of different types were aimed at obtaining greater artistic quality and more suitable decoration of the articles.

Metal jewellery gave greater brilliance to the costumes made of fabrics: pins, forehead ornaments, earrings, *kossichniks,* necklaces, belt buckles, bracelets and rings were commonly worn. They were used in moderation, but still in sufficient quantities to give the costumes a festive touch. Some of these metal ornaments were obviously primarily practical accessories, while others were constructive elements, but in material, and particularly in form, workmanship and ornamentation they gradually became real jewellery. Belt buckles, for instance, belong to the first group, serving in the past as they do today, to fasten belts, but they became pieces of jewellery because of the brilliance of the silver and the gilding, the many colours of enamel, the relief of the wrought or cast surfaces, the dainty web of filigree, and with their round, oblong of palmette forms. There ist great variety in the coin ornaments which usually cover fairly large areas on hats, breast pieces, etc.

But their use was not accidental, or an end in itself. They were usually organically linked with the costumes, having a definite place of them and forming a constructive element in the com-

155
Woman's everyday summer costume. Pleven region. Late 19th century. Painting by Ivan Mrkvička.

156
Woman's summer festive costume. Pleven region. Late 19th century.

157
Girl's festive costume. Pleven region. Late 19th century. Painting by Ivan Mrkvička.

155

156

157

plete composition of the costume.

Bulgarian national costumes were also supplemented by ornaments which varied in form and material. Ornaments made of materials found ready to hand in the environment, such as flowers, feathers and fibres, were widely used and gave a fresh touch and colour to them, as well as variety to their forms. Some of them were prototypes of the later metal jewellery.

Regardless of their artistic effect, the ornamented fabrics, embroideries, laces, appliqué work, edgings and even the jewellery and ornaments were not merely decorative elements. They played an essential role in the complete structure of the costumes. In its early stage as a decorative seam, embroidery determined the basic lines of the garments, while its edges appeared as a logical framework for it. Those parts of the embroidery which helped to emphasize definite forms on a separate garment, or on the whole costume, underwent artistic development. The trapeze shape of the skirts of women's outer garments was emphasized by concentrating the linear decoration of edgings at the top of the insets on both sides of the waist. The straight lines of the *soukmans* in the Samokov, Sofia and other regions of Western Bulgaria were intensified by embroidering small patterns on them with a rhythmical change of colour. In other cases the position of the embroidery, even its patterns and colours helped to achieve exquisite outlines. The position of almost all embroidered decoration was conditioned by the basic characteristics of the whole composition of the costumes. Embroideries worked on the national costumes combined their decorative purpose with the purposes of the costumes' structure, and always did so successfully.

Embroidery also appeared as a uniting link between the separate parts of the costume in a complete and harmonious combination.

158
Girl's head ornament. Pleven region. Late 19th century.

159
Young bride's festive costume. Pleven region. Late 19th century.

160
Young bride's festive costume. Pleven region. Late 19th century.

158

159

160

161

162

163

164

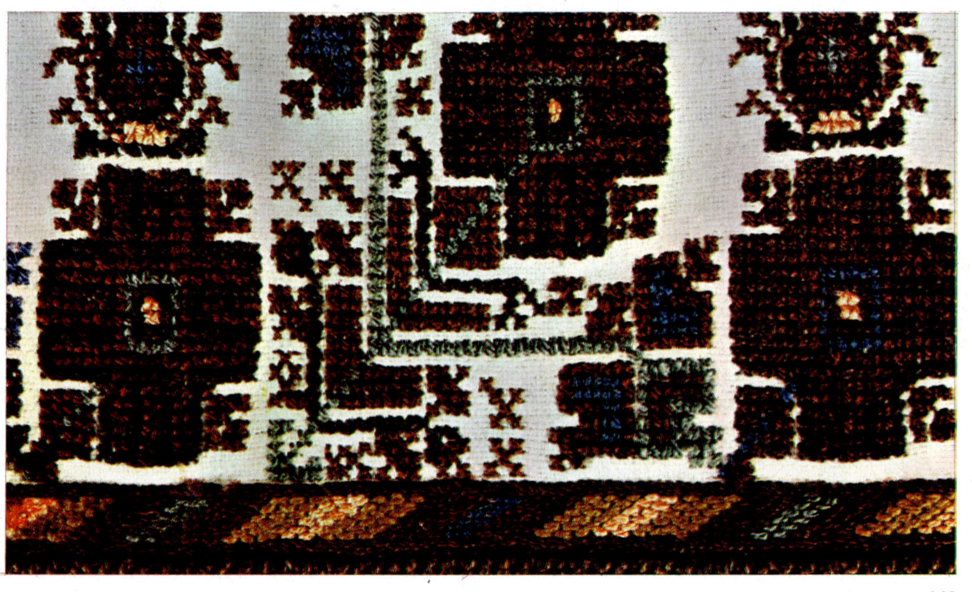
165

161
Head scarf and ornamentation as worn by a young bride. Pleven region. Late 19th century.

162
Embroidery on the sleeve of a woman's chemise. Pleven region. Second half of the 19th century.

163
Embroidery along the front opening of a woman's chemise. Pleven region. Late 19th century.

164
Embroidery on the hem of a woman's chemise. Pleven region. Late 19th century.

165
Embroidery on the hem of a woman's chemise. Pleven region. Late 19th century.

BASIC TYPES OF COSTUMES AND LOCAL VARIANTS

The extraordinary variety of costumes found in Bulgaria developed from the basic one, which possessed the essential features, under the influence of a number of factors of different characters: historical, geographical, economic, social, cultural and aesthetic. In Bulgarian ethnography several indicators are accepted, on the basis of which the traditional national costumes were differentiated into several types with a definite geographical distribution and original historical development.

The shape and colour of men's and women's upper garments were among the principal marks by which the distribution was noted, since it was these garments which determined the aspect of the costumes. Women's costumes are divided into four groups, according to the cut and manner of wearing upper garments: the *soukman,* two-apron, one-apron and *saya* types. According to the shape of the upper garments and the colour of the fabrics used in making them the men's costumes are differentiated into two groups: *belodreshni* (white clothes) and *chernodreshni* (black clothes) costumes.

Of the basic women's types of costumes, the *soukman* type has proved to be the most widespread and the most resistant to change.

The *soukman* costume has as its basic garment a long whole chemise over which the *soukman* is worn, held in by a belt, and with an apron tied over it. The chemise of the *soukman costume* is like a tunic in cut, composed of one piece of fabric of double length from shoulder to ankles, folded in two, with an opening for the head, widened by insets at the sides and having wide open sleeves. Only in regions in which both the two-apron and the *soukman* type of costumes are worn is the *soukman* combined with the *burchanka* (gathered) type of chemise. The embroidery which decorates the costume is concentrated along the edges: the collar, the front opening, the sleeve edges, and often along the middle of their front part and the skirts. The *soukman* is made of linen, hempen or cotton fabric, but most often of black or dark blue woollen material, like a tunic in cut, long, closed, sleeveless or with short and rarely with long sleeves, with insets at the sides from the underarm or the waist, and in the Eastern regions one finds a *soukman* composed of a short sleeveless bodice and a gathered skirt.

Each of these principal variants has many local ones, according to the decoration of the garment, which consists of linear, multicoloured or one colour embroidery, for instance, on the short-inset *soukmans* of the Sofia region, along the edges of the front opening, the ends of the sleeves and the insets. The characteristic decoration of a *soukman* with high insets is embroidery and appliqué work at the hems of the skirts. White embroidery and stitching along the ends and seams stand out against the dark background of the *soukman.* The apron of the *soukman* costume is in almost all variants a decorative centre because of its rich and multi-coloured ornamentation. A wide waistband in bright colours or a belt, is a necessary accessory to the *soukman* costume. When complete, this costume also has outer garments of different cut and colour, and is connected with a variety of hair-dos and ways of wearing the head scarf: *nalessa* (many braids merging into one) or

166
Woman's outer garment. Pleven region. Second half of 19th century.

166

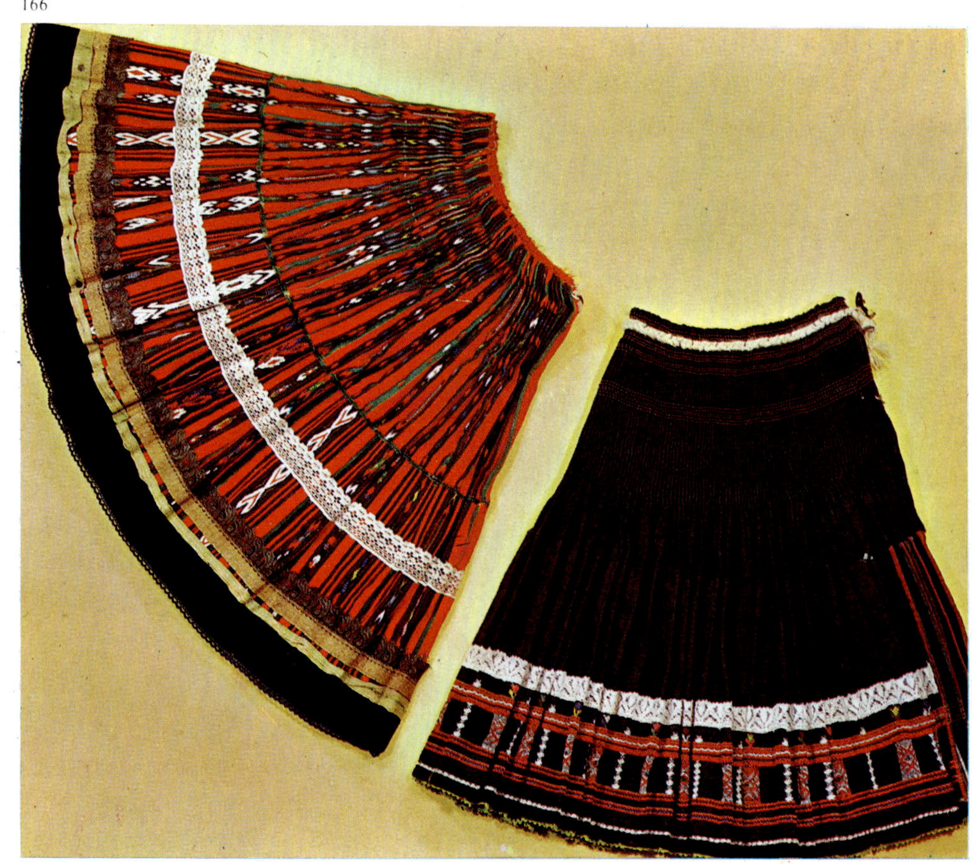

in numerous plaits hanging down the back, supplemented with wreaths and *kosichniks,* various adjuncts to footwear: stockings, or *kaltsouni* made of fabric, *lapchouni,* and *terlitsi.*

The *soukman* type of costume was worn in the central regions of the country, and chiefly in the mountainous parts: Stara Planina, The Sredna Gora region, around Vitosha Mountain. the Rila Mountains, the Central Rhodopes, the Strandja Uplands and South-Eastern Thrace. It was everywhere worn all the year round, except on the northern slopes of Stara Planina, where it alternated as winter wear with the two-apron costume. It became more widespread at the cost of the other types of costumes because it was perfected as a garment and also because of the movement of its wearers from the centres towards regions where other costumes were worn, for economic, historical and other reasons.

A chemise and two aprons were the basic articles of wear in the *two-apron costume.* The chemise was usually of the *burchanka* type, gathered around the neckline, in some variants also at the top and end of the sleeves, with a shoulder inset between the principal pieces of fabric; this inset was triangular or trapeze-shaped, actually square, but with a gathered upper edge. Only in some regions, such as the Vidin region, for instance, at the village of Novo Selo and other villages, in Razgrad, Popovo, Preslav and Provadiya regions, the two-apron costume consisted of a tunic-shaped chemise, long, straight, without gathers and with

167

Ornamentation on a woman's outer garment. Pleven region. Second half of 19th century.

168

Back skirts from Pleven region. Late 19th century.

167

168

169

170

wide and open sleeves. The apron worn with this costume was made of decorative fabrics possessing different artistic qualities, made of one or two widths of the fabric, joined together horizontally or vertically. The back skirts appeared in many variants which can, nevertheless, be divided into three groups: a skirt made of ornamental fabric, most often in red, gathered or pleated, found chiefly in North-Western Bulgaria; another of dark blue or black fabric with a coloured border at the lower edge, predominant in Central North Bulgaria; a skirt made of black fabric, gathered or pleated, but with embroidery at the hem, worn in North-Eastern Bulgaria. Usually the three variants of the *burchanka* chemise coincided with the three variants of back skirts, owing to which three regions were differentiated in Northern Bulgaria: in North-Western Bulgaria, a *burchanka* chemise with small triangular shoulder insets and a *vulnenik or bruchnik* (as the back skirt was called there) of ornamented fabric, a one- or two-width apron with a horizontal seam; in Central Northern Bulgaria, it was worn with a *borka* chemise, gathered at the top of the sleeves and a *peshtemal* (back skirt) of blue fabric with a narrow border along the skirt edge and a richtly ornamented apron with a perpendicular seam; in North-Eastern Bulgaria, a chemise with large *altitsi* (insets under the armhole) and a back skirt of black fabric with embroidery, a two-width apron with a perpendicular seam and slight gathers at the upper end; its ornamentation was concentrated a long the lower edge.

A belt was also part of the basic composition of the two-apron costume, usually woven *na kori,* richly ornamented with strips of different colours or motifs, forming a chain along its length.

White outer garments strikingly ornamented with linear embroidery and appliqué work at the tops of the insets on both sides of the

169
Young men in festive summer costumes Pleven region. Late 19th century.

170
Woman's *borka* chemise. Lovech region. Second half of the 19th century.

171

Everyday costume for a young woman. Lovech region. Second half of 19th century. Painting by Ivan Mrkvička.

172

Embroidery on the sleeve of a woman's chemise. Lovech region. Second half of the 19th century.

173

Embroidery on the hem of a woman's chemise. Lovech regon. Second half of the 19th century.

back completed a bride's costume in these regions.

A variety of hair-dos and ornaments for girls, special ways of wearing the head scarf for brides, and also special footwear were linked with the two-apron costume. The most frequent hair-do for a girl consisted of numerous plaits, beginning at the side of the head and gradually merging into one plait, ornamented with wreaths and *kossichniks* shaped like the natural hair-do. A bride wore her head scarf, which consisted of a long piece of cloth or a square, over horn-shaped or semi-circular or round pads.

Ethnographic research carried out so far has establised that the women's two-apron costume was worn chiefly in Northern Bulgaria, from the River Timok to Silistra and from the northern slopes of Stara Planina to the Danube. In this extensive region it was the only wear mainly in the villages along the Danube, along the lower reaches of the Rivers Vit, Ossum, Yantra, Roussenski Lom and in the Silistra region. In the remaining regions particularly in the foothills of Stara Planina, it was seasonal wear the summer costume being replaced by the *soukman* costume in winter.

The *saya* costume also has a tunic-shaped chemise as its basic component, and the *saya* as its upper garment; this is a long garment, open down the front, with short or long sleeves. There are several variantsof the*saya,* with a definite geographical distribution and, of course with several local variants. In the Pirin region a *saya* made of fabrics in one colour, white or blue, predominated; it was knee-length slightly flared, ornamented with linear embroidery around the front opening and the ends of the sleeves. In the other centre of the *saya* costume – the Kyustendil region – the *saya* was also made of a fabric in one colour, black, dark green or white, of medium length ornamented around the neck line and at

174

175

the sleeve ends with coloured braid. One of its widespread variants, chiefly along the middle reaches of the River Maritsa, was made of striped multi-coloured fabric (the stripes were along the warp); this *saya* was almost ankle length, had wide insets and long sleeves. Aprons and a waistband, ornamented in different ways, head scarves and footwear belong to these variants. The apron was usually made of a striped fabric with the exception of the Pirin region, and was less decorative than those worn with the two-apron and *soukman* costumes.

The *saya* costume was worn chiefly in the southern regions of the country. It is one of the basic types of costumes which continues to be worn even in our own day by the population, adapted to the new conditions of life and to the aesthetic requirements of the present.

The one-apron costume was the simplest in composition; it consisted of a long chemise over which an apron was tied, made of one narrow width of cloth, as in Blagoevgrad and Zlatograd, or of a broad two-width apron which covered the whole lower part of the body, as it was worn in Velingrad and other places. This costume had the most limited, inconstant and short life. It was maintained chiefly in the Western and Eastern Rhodopes. It was worn in this form chielfy at home or at work in the fields, and on festive occasions turned into the *saya* form, being worn with an open upper garment, when travelling or taking part in any celebrations.

The two types of men's costumes were not geographical variants, but two consecutive stages in the development of men's costumes. A man's summer costume as a farmer in Northern Bulgaria and the Pirin region is accepted as their origin; it consisted of a long shirt, worn over the trousers with a waistband wound around it; this costume still bore traces of the costume worn by the Slavs in

174
Embroidered ends of a woman's head scarf. Lovech region. Early 19th century.

175
Embroidered end of a woman's head scarf. Lovech region. Early 19th century.

176
Apron from Lovech region. Late 19th century.

176

177
Belt from Lovech region. Late 19th century.

177

178
Embroidery on the hem of a woman's chemise. Lovech region. Second half of the 19th century.

178

olden times, but it was preserved in these regions up to the early years of the 20 th century mainly owing to its suitability for work in the fields.

The old white-garment costume worn by men consisted of a tunic-like shirt, trousers and an outer garment of white felted woollen material. The trousers worn with this costume belonged to two of the principal types: *benevretsi* with long and narrow trouser legs, and *dimii* with short and wide trouser legs, worn with white puttees. The silhoeutte of the white-garment costume owed its principal features to the shape of its upper garments. They were either a little more than waist-length or reached down to the knees and below them; they were open down the front, slightly flared and ornamented with coloured edgings or braiding in red, blue and black, along the seams, the front opening and the top of the insets. A waistband, striped in many colours or else with its front end richly ornamented was worn with this costume. There were three variants of these upper garments, depending on the length of the sleeves, some having long and some elbow length sleeves, and some none at all. A semi-spherical fur hat was an almost constant accessory of this cosume, worn in the past over a red skull cap or 'under hat'; blunt tipped sandals of tanned or un-tanned pig- or ox-skin were the usual footwear.

The old White-garment men's costume was preserved for the longest time in the Western regions of the country; however, it has today almost completely disappeared as ordinary wear, being usually replaced by clothes of the type worn in towns.

In certain Western regions a transitional form between the white-garment and the black-garment costumes was worn for a fairly long time.

In the regions of Sofia, Samokov, Stankedimitrov and Kyustendil

179

Young woman's everyday costume. Svishtov region. Late 19th century.

180

Young women's festive costumes. Svishtov region. Late 19th century.

179

180

the men's costumes worn up to the early years of the 20th century were a combination of white trousers, *benevretsi,* and a dark upper garment in blue or the natural colour of the wool; in form it was like the old white garment, open down the front, coming down below the waist in length, with small insets, and linear ornamentation along the edges of the front and the insets. A more advanced stage in the transition to town clothes was marked by costumes of dark homespun which kept to the cut and shape characteristic of the whitegarment costume; the costumes of the Belené and Plovdiv regions were worn with trousers called *burdentsi* of blue fabric, while in the region of Provadiya, men's costumes were made of black fabric with narrow trousers and a short-sleeved jacket.

The typical black-garment costume was given this name chiefly because of the dark colour of the fabric used for the upper garments; it inherited from the white-garment costume the shirt, cut like a tunic; in more recent times this was replaced by a shirt which had a yoke at the shoulders. There were, however, considerable differences in the cut and form of the trousers and the upper garments and hence in the whole silhouette of the costumes. The trousers were wide and gathered at the waist with gradually narrowing trouserlegs, and pockets cut into the sides. The upper garments were waistlength, open down the front, but straight in line, sleeveless or more often with long sleeves. They were braided along the seams and edges, and this braiding often became very decorative with linear ornaments around the edges of the garments. A wide red waistband was worn with the black-garment costume, wound around the waist. The remaining parts of the costume – hat, footwear, etc., were usually like the elements of the white-garment costume.

181

Women's festive costumes. Nikopol region. Late 19th century.

182

Embroidery on the front of a man's shirt. Nikopol region. Late 19th century.

183

Embroideries on the sleeve of a man's shirt. Nikopol region. Late 19th century.

181

182

183

184

The black-garment costume, resulting from the commodity production of homespuns in the National Revival period, gradually flooded the country from the East and the South to the West and the North, where it replaced the old white-garment costume, until this form itself yielded pride of place to the type of clothes worn in towns. Even up to the mid-19th century it was worn in farm work and animal husbandry, chiefly in Eastern and South-Eastern Bulgaria, by old people, because it was comfortable and convenient.

184
Everyday summer costume worn by a young woman. Belené region Early 20th century.

As already said, there were no strict boundaries to the geographic distribution of the principal types of costumes. There were intermediary zones between them in which clothing with elements taken from both costumes were worn, the one or the other predominating. A typical example is provided by the common use of the two-apron and the *soukman* costume along the northern foothills of Stara Planina. The *soukman* costumes in the region of the Rila Mountains shared a common silhouette with the *saya* costumes, because of their proximity, and this even spread to the position of the ornamentation, the type of apron and waistband worn. On the other hand, the one-apron costume passed over to the *saya* type in many villages and along many groups of the population.

Each of these basic types of costume were subdivided into *variants* in the outer form of the garments, the manner of wearing

185

186

185
Young woman in summer costume from Roussé region. Late 19th century. Painting by Ivan Mrkvička.

186
Girl wearing a festive summer costume. Roussé region. Late 19th century.

them and particularly the workmanship and artistry which went into them. These variants were usually to be found in regions which were differentiated by geographic and economic conditions. Each local variant numbered many sub-variants in the more remote districts.

The *soukman* costume offers a particularly great variety. The old costumes of Znepolé and Graovo had a white hempen *manofil* (a children's *soukman)* decorated with much embroidery; or a blue cloth *soukman* was worn in winter, quite different from the neighbouring costumes worn in the Sofia Plain, where a dark cloth *soukman* ornamented with embroidery worked in white was the rule, or from the costumes worn in the high Samokov Plain, where the chemises were ornamented with multi-coloured embroidery around the front opening, the short sleeves and the hems. There are countless variants of the *soukman* costumes in the Stara Planina Mountains, the Sredna Gora region and Thrace, as regards the decoration of the *soukmans* – appliqué work or embroidery on the skirts to a height of from 7 to 8 cm up to 50 to 60 cm, such as, for instance, in the Stara Zagora, Yambol, Sevlievo, Gabrovo, Sliven and Karnobat regions. Thus, for instance, the two-apron costume numbers many variants which were chiefly differentiated along the valleys of the Rivers Timok, Lom, Ogosta, Isker, Vit, Ossum, Yantra and Roussenski Lom. These variants were differentiated not only in the details of the cut of the *burchanka* chemise in its three types, and the tunic-shaped chemise; in the outer form of the back skirt such as the *vulnenik, bruchnik, peshtemal* and *kurlyanka,* but even in the shades of the colours. For instance, in the different regions from West to East red varies from a delicate rose colour to a dark crimson; green ranges from the spring green to dark green; blue from sky blue to navy blue, etc.

The *saya* costume appears in a considerable number of variants in the three larger regions in which it is worn: *sayas* made of striped fabrics in the valley of the River Maritsa and in the Rhodopes; a white or blue *saya* and at some places a striped *saya* in the Pirin region; a black or dark green *saya* for winter and a white one for summer with gold thread embroidery and coloured braiding in the Kyustendil and Radomir regions.

Even the one-apron costume, though more limited in distribution, also had several variants.

The men's white-garment costume appeared chiefly in two variants – with white *benevretsi* (trousers with narrow and long legs) in Western Bulgaria, and with *dimii,* which have short and wide trouser legs, in Central North Bulgaria and the Pirin region. The black-garment costume, on the other hand, which displaced the white-garment costume as early as the National Revival period, moving from East to West, had many variants, due to the shades of the dark woollen cloth of which the upper garments were made, the cut of the waistcoats and quilted jackets and the designs of the braiding.

The variety of traditional costumes was not restricted to regions, and not even to outskirts, but to individual villages. At inter-village celebrations and fairs, the inhabitants of individual villages recognized one another's origin by the design of the fabrics

187

Young woman's festive winter costume. Roussé region. Late 19th century.

188

Bachelor's festive costume. Roussé region. Late 19th century.

189

Girl's festive costume. Roussé region. Early 20th century.

187

188

189

for aprons, back skirts, *soukmans* and *sayas,* belts and waistbands, by the patterns and colours of the embroideries and knitwear, by the way they were worn, by the ways women wore their head scarves, their jewellery and footwear. No two identical costumes were to be found in one and the same village, because every woman who used to make the garments in the past, put something of her own, something very personal into her work, whereby she enriched the common fund of clothing, renewing and varying it. Even in a bride's chest no two costumes were alike, each one being a separate work of art for her, the fruit of different creative inspirations and emotions, but the unique features of a national costume, common to the Bulgarian people, were always to be found in them.

The costumes worn when rites and customs were being performed, with their special accessories, increased the variety of garments worn though only temporarily.

The great variety found in Bulgarian national costumes is largely due to the art that went into their making, and the population of various regions added to this variety by their aesthetic norms. According to th aesthetic demands of the population of North Western Bulgaria the two-apron costume had to have straight lines; that is why the chemise was made of hempen fabric, and the back skirt *(vulnenik)* had to be made of a thickly woven woollen fabric, so that it would not cling to the hempen chemise, but stick out at the back. On the other hand, the costume worn in the Vidin and Belogradchik regions was more fan-shaped in line: the *vulnenik* was finely gathered and spread out like a fan; the chemise was also finely gathered around the neckline, and even the embroidered head scarf was finely pleated. A more rounded look was typical of the costumes in Roussé district: the chemise,

190

Man's and woman's festive costumes. Roussé region. Early 20th century.

191

Dancing the bouyenets. Roussé region. Early 20th century.

190

191

192

193

the *kurlyanka* (back skirt) and the apron were all freely gathered. According to the taste of the women of the Sofia, Samokov and Stankedimitrov regions, the *soukman* had to be worn with the insets pushed to the back. In Thrace the *soukmans* were worn with soft folds placed regularly along the whole width of the skirts. The *aladjas* and *sayas* worn along the valley of the River Maritsa also had to be worn with the side insets drawn towards the back, which made them look like wings. There were different ways of wearing waistbands, tying on the aprons at diferrent places, and individual garments were also worn in different ways. In North Western Bulgaria, particularly in the most north-western regions, the waistband which was not very wide, was very tightly wound round the waist, while the men of Thrace wore a broad waistband which even covered part of the chest. The women of Sliven let the ties of their apron hang down the back, thus introducing one more decorative element into the back part of their costumes. The women of Ihtiman, for their part, tied their aprons at the side, and as they were quite wide, like ribbons, they stood out against the single colour of the apron in form and contrasting colour. In certain parts of Kurdjali region the girls tied on their aprons in different ways – at the side, back or front. The detailed care given to the women's appearance even went so far as regulating the line on the forehead at which the head scarf was to be worn – low down over the foredead, or high up, revealing part of the hair. Particular attention was paid to colour combinations between the different parts of the costume. For instance, according to established artistic requrments in the Strandja Uplands a red apron was best suited to the white skirt or *grizh (type* of *soukman).* According to the women of the Dobroudja, the beauty of a costume was chiefly due to the contrasting colours of the dress and the apron – a red

192

Girl in *Bouyenets* costume. dressed to take part in the Lazarus Day dances. Roussé region. Late 19th century.

193

Girl in *bouyenets* costume. Silistra region. late 19th century.

194
Girl's festive costume. Razgrad region. Late 19th century.

195
Embroidery on the sleeve of a woman's chemise. Razgrad region. Early 20th century.

dress had to be worn with a black apron and vice versa, a red apron went with a dark coloured dress. For the girls and women in the village of Kozichino, near Pomorié, the ideal combination was a black *soukman* and a *crooked apron,* made up of perpendicular black and white stripes.

In the separate villages of the Vidin, Belogradchik, Botevgrad and the Teteven, Lovech and Pleven regions the population was differentiated by the width of the stripes and the predominant motifs on the weaves of aprons and back skirts; in Sevlievo, Nikopol, Svishtov and Belené regions, it was the distinctive decorative elements along the border of the *peshtemal* (form of back skirt worn in these regions), which indicated which particular village they came from; in Roussé district, it was the shade of the orangey-red colour of the embroideries on the chemise and the *kurlyanka* (back skirt) which identified the village; in Sliven and Yambol regions - the patterns on the fabrics of the dresses, the ornaments on the aprons; in Karnobat region – the outer form of a bride's hood; in the Stara Zagora, Nova Zagora and Elhovo regions – the order in which the strips of coloured cloth were placed along the bottom of the *soukman,* the ornaments on the aprons, etc. When the force of one of the laws governing the artistic formation of the costumes is borne in mind, the law of harmoniously combining the individual parts of the costumes, it becomes clear that differences in the whole costumes must also appear. There is no village in the country in which a costume, exactly similar to one worn in any other village, near or far, is to be found.

Besides the essential factors, such as conditions of labour and way of life, depending on the environment, economic development, character and style of the artistic form given to them, a number of other factors played a part in the unique variety of components found in the composition of Bulgarian national costumes. For instance, the originality of certain local Bulgaran costumes can be explained as traces of *cultural and historical strata,* manifested to various degrees in various regions, and in the different stage of their development. In certain local costumes, particularly those connected with rites and customs, traces of the earliest stages of human culture can be observed, having passed over to the Bulgarians through the Indo-European community; these features have shown different degrees of stability in different regions. To these features belong the different ornaments and accessories made of materials found to hand, such as flowers, barks, seeds, fibres, etc.

The degree to which they were influenced by the culture of clothing in the Mediterranean cultural region in Antiquity and the Middle Ages, is apparent in the cut of certain garments, the way the ornaments are placed, etc. To this is due the variety of the elements which form the costumes, particularly those worn by women.

A number of deviations from the basic specific features of the tradtitional costumes should be attributed to *the variety of the Slav foundation* on which they developed. The Slav elements, the presence of which has been proved in Bulgarian national costumes, show that the Slavs brought to the Balkans garments made in different ways: pieces of fabric joined in different ways on

196

196
Embroidery on an apron from Razgrad region. Early 20th century.

the shoulders, as in the *burchanka* (gathered) chemise; slipping the garment over the head, as in the tunic-shaped chemises and shirts; tying around the waist as aprons and back skirts; folding to the back or sides, as in the other garments ad the *sayas;* closed garments slipped on, as for the feet, etc. Various forms of garments and costumes became established in different regions under the influence of essential and secondary factors. Certain Slav garments served to shape new garments worn in other ways, forming complete new costumes. The *soukman* offers a strik i ng example of this; it is considered that it doubles the basic garment, but developing locally, it formed a new costume composition. In Bulgaria different stages in forming the basic compositions are to be seen. For instance, the *soukman* costume of Znepolé and Graovo have *manofils* which are an almost complete repetition of the chemise in material, cut and ornamentation; the *soukman* costumes, with insets placed high up at the sides, were made of white fabrics woven from yarns of plant origin and in their natural colour, but they had no sleeves, which would get in the way of their movements when working, as is the case in the costumes of the Strandja Uplands; the costums in which the *soukman* is made of woollen fabric in natural colours, as worn around Ihtiman in the 16th century; others richly ornamented with embroidery and appliqué work, as worn in Thrace, the Stara Planina, the Sredna Gora region, and the Valley of Roses; the *soukman* costumes with

197

Young women's everyday costumes. Kyustendil region. Early 20th century.

197

198

199

short insets, cut on the bias, as in Sofia region, all mark different stages in the development of the *soukman.*

However, even in this period of the destruction of traditional clothing under pressure from capitalist production, new costumes appeared to enrich the variety of Bulgarian costumes. They were usually due to the technical improvement of some of the work in making them, such as weaving, knitting, sewing, shoemaking, etc. In this period costumes appeared in which one-colour fabrics for the *soukmans* and *sayas* were replaced by fabrics for upper garments in a variety of weaves and designs, the technical workmanship of which shows a higher stage of development. The costumes of the regions of Sliven, Yambol, Karnobat, Varna, Provadiya, the Dobroudja, etc., are typical examples of this; here, instead of the old black *soukman* dresses made of handwoven fabrics in various colours, chiefly red, striped or checked, began to be worn; they consisted of a bodice and a gathered skirt. In this period again striped silk *soukmans* (red and black, green and black, blue and white) began to be worn. In Razlog region, the new skirt, made of pure black woollen closely woven material finely pleated, and attached to a bodice, displaced the old *saya* costume. In a number of villages along the River Maritsa a gathered skirt and a bodice began to be made of the fabrics formerly used for *sayas.* These new costumes show how improved technology became the foundation for essential changes in clothing, and for its advance. The new fabrics, which owed their existence to improved technology, made it possible to give new forms to clothes which consequently marked an advance. These new costumes, appearing under circumstances which oppressed the people, proved the vitality of their creative urges and the constant improvement of their skill; it also showed that they were eager to find new and more progressive and artistic forms.

198

Woman's festive winter costume. Kyustendil region. Second half of the 19th century. Painting by Ivan Mrkvička.

199

Embroideries on the sleeve of a woman's chemise. Kyustendil region. Second half of the 19th century.

200 201 202

200

Ornamentation on the breast edges and sleeves of a *saya* (woman's upper garment). Kyustendil region. Late 19th century.

201

Ornamentation on the sleeve ends of a *saya*. Kyustendil region. Early 20th century.

202

Woman's costume. Razlog region. Early 20th century.

203
Fabric for an apron. Razlog region. Early 20th century.

204
Girl's costume. Razlog region. Late 19th century. Painting by Ivan Mrkvička.

205
Fabric for an apron. Bansko region. Late 19th century.

203

204

205

FUNCTION

A considerable part of the variety found in the traditional national costumes is due to the fact that they expressed social relationships.

Traces of marks, showing relationships, and inherent in the clan-communal structure of society can be discovered in the traditional costumes. They indicated differences in age, family status, etc., and although their initial meaning faded and has even been forgotten, they have retained because of their artistic qualities, or simply by force of habit. Marks of social relationships in a class society were also apparent in them, such as material condition, social affiliation, service or rank in a professional and public organization, etc. These marks were most often visible superficially, and were noticeable in ornamentation and colour, but some of them also affected fabric, cut and the elements of a costume.

Since at the time when costumes took shape *the age* of the persons who wore them was considered an important indicator of their place and the part they played in society, it strongly influenced clothing. The people differentiated costumes for every age, from childhood to extreme old age. The age factor mainly affected the outward side of costumes — material, manner of preparation, components, hair-do and manner in which the head scarf was worn, more particularly textile ornamentation, colour scheme, design of the ornamentation. For instance, at the marrigeable age, before marriage and also in the first years after it, a woman's costume was at the height of its beauty. Many elements enriched the costumes of girls of marriageable age, fiancées or young brides; in most cases they were decorative in character, being apparent in form and colour, and creating an impression of festivity. After this period the costumes gradually began to be rid of elements which were unnecessary from a practical point of view, until those worn by the very aged were reduced to the basic elements.

Embroideries on the chemises worn in some of the villages in the Danubian Plain offer a typical example of the differences in the decoration of costumes worn by women of different ages. Chemises worn by little girls of 10 to 12 years of age had a pale ornament in the weave of the fabric at the top of the sleeves. At the ages of 13 and 14, little girls already had two stripes of embroidery on both sides of the woven motif, all down the length of the sleeve. Girls of 15 and 16 wore chemises with brightly coloured embroidery in a rectangular motif, with two embroidered stripes down the whole front of the sleeves. Before their marriage girls wore chemises with the richest ornamentation, known as *purki,* a broad stripe down the whole sleeve front. This was a distinctive feature for young brides too. Age was shown by a cross at the top of the sleeves and pale colours in one shade in the embroidery of the skirt. In other regions, regardless of the family status, girls and brides wore garments ornamented in the same way in their youth. For instance, in the region where the *soukman* costume was worn, the young women wore this garment ornamented with applications of light coloured strips along the hems, while the old women had motifs embroidered in dark colours on theirs (in Yambol, Stara Zagora, Nova Zagora and Kazanluk regions), or only in one colour, most often a white embroidered line at a definite height (Elhovo and Groudovo). Many other, often strange ways of showing age are found, ways which the population in various parts of the country established for their garments.

Age was not so clearly marked in the men's costumes. The difference in age between old and young was chiefly shown in the decoration of the garments they wore, mainly in the edgings, in the colour of the separate parts, such as the waistband, and in the presence of supplementary elements, ways in which the garments were worn , etc. The costumes of bachelors and young men, even when married, was distinguished by comparatively rich ornamentation of the edgings, particularly around the pockets, on both sides of the front. Embroidery in the shirts was used as proof of their age, and the lads of Sliven district, for instance, at least on holidays wore a shirt with multi-coloured embroidery all over the front of the sleeves, while the old men wore only white shirts. The colour of the waistband was a distinctive sign of age. Young men wore bright colours, and a dark waistband was typical for the old men. Another sign of youth was the leather belt, covered with metal studs, and the richly ornamented handkerchiefs thrust into the waistband or worn around the neck; a young man always wore his fur hat jauntily stuck on one side; his puttees were tightly wound and the black woollen strings or leather straps, which held them in place, stood out in intricate patterns against the white cloth.

206

206

Girl's spring costume. Sandanski region. Early 20th century.

The family is the fundamental nucleus of society among the Bulgarians and the place and role of every member of it were strictly determined. The family status of persons was also reflected in clothing. However, as in other indicators, women's costumes were sensitive in this respect, as in this case, when compared with the men's costumes, and that is why they showed greater variety. Here again differences were apparent in the component of the costumes, the forms of individual garments, the manner in which they were worn, their ornamentation, and more particularly the hair-dos and the way in which the head scarf was worn. A woman's situation in the family whether she was a girl, engaged to be married, a bride, a mother, a mother-in-law or a widow, was indicated in detail by the clothes she wore. A girl's costume, for instance, even though it had reached its full development as far as decoration was concerned, lacked outer garments. They were the privilege of married women only. Girls embroidered their white garments before they married, but they had no right to wear them. The wearing of an outer garment indicated the married state. Old women still remember the intolerable heat when they worked in the fields as young brides and were obliged to wear their short white jackets and long coats with elbow-length sleeves. In the region of the Rila mountains the married women wore red waistbands as a distinctive feature. In the Sofia region sleeves, the fronts of which were not embroidered, showed that their wearers were unmarried. But a bride's sleeves were beautifully embroidered in raspberry red silks. Even details of a woman's family status were shown by the ornamentation of her clothes. In Thrace, the region around Sliven, Yambol, Karnobat, Elhovo, Topolovgrad and Groudovo, from the day of their marriage, during the first months and even years of their married life, young brides wore *soukmans* which were bordered by scarlet strips of hand woven cotton, or woollen fabrics, or red silk.

But it was the hair-do and the manner of wearing the head scarf which most clearly indicated the family status of a woman. Uncovered hair was the principal sign of girlhood, and the white head scarf which covered her hair most clearly indicated a bride. In the hair-dos there were sometimes almost unnoticeable details which indicated a bride or a girl, for instance, a girl would braid her hair into odd-numbered braids, while a bride's braids were even-numbered. In places where head scarves were worn at a later age by girls, there were differences in their colour as well as in the way they were worn. A white head scarf remained the privilege of the bride, while girls wore coloured head scarves which were looked upon more as a decorative element.

Garments also showed the transition from one family status to another. The costume of a girl who was engaged to be married was worn with metal jewellery, usually the gift of her fiancé. 'If you looked down from the crags, you would know which of the girls was engaged, she glittered so,' old women will tell you, remembering the rich garb of engaged girls at the village of Banichan, Gotsedelchev district. Among the population of the Dobroudja a piece of jewellery called *askii,* consisting of small chains, decorated with rhomboid platelets, their ends gathered together in the two angles of a triangle or a sphere, and

207

Embroidery on the sleeves and hem of a woman's chemise. Sandanski region. Late 19th century.

208

Embroidery on the sleeves and hem of a woman's chemise. Sandanski region. Late 19th century.

207

208

worn over the head scarf, indicated that a girl was engaged. Wedding costumes, in their full rig and rich decoration, were strictly established and kept to. They consisted of the most richly embroidered chemises and *soukmans,* the most impressive outer garments, multi-coloured aprons thickly covered with ornaments, belts and waistbands. Accessories further enriched them and were eloquent features, distinguishing a bridal couple.

The costume also showed the young woman's entry into one of the most important periods of her life – motherhood. In many places the form and elements of the hair-do and manner of wearing the head scarf also showed essential changes when a woman became a mother. A mother was expected not to wear much jewellery. A mother who had reared her children and seen them married, particularly her sons, could not wear garments with certain definite ornaments.

The men's costumes did not so markedly indicate their family status and age as the women's did. There was not much difference in the clothes worn by bachelors and young married men. Only in some places were insignificant differences retained until fairly late.

On the other hand, signs showing social position and profession were very strictly marked on men's costumes. They were chiefly apparent in the quality of the material, the quantity and effectiveness of the ornamentation and the composition of the costume. These features were even apparent in the old white-garment costumes. The costume which required long and narrow *benevretsi* was worn mostly by poor farmers, shepherds and lumbermen, while the affluent wore the short and wide *dimii.* During the National Revival period, in the commodity production centres of Kotel, Karlovo, Kalofer, Klissoura and Etropolé, the poor

209
Apron from Gotsedelchev region. Late 19th century.

209

210

and even more well-to-do farmers, shepherds and craftsmen wore rather narrow *potouri* (full-bottomed breeches) with a single row of braiding; the affluent guild members and merchants wore wider *potouri* more richly ornamented with braiding, while the *chorbadjis,* as the rich notables were called, wore extravagantly long and full *shalvari* (baggy trousers). A silk waistband, striped in many colours, belonged to the *chorbadji'* s costume; he also wore an *anteria* (quilted jacket) which was either made of silk or of material brought from the Eastern markets, soft leather shoes, a gold chain for his watch and a red fez. The craftsman, who was a guild member, wore a red woollen belt with his costume, a short jacket with fur edgings down the front, an astrakhan hat, white stockings and shallow shoes, called *eminii.* The costumes worn by the poor shepherds, ploughmen and craftsmen seemed to have been poured out of homespun frieze in the natural colour of the wool, and worn with a woollen waistband, often undyed, the upper garments braided with edging along the seams, placed there mainly for practical purposes, white leggings and leather sandals. The signs which indicated a woman's social position, or to be more precise, that of her family, were apparent in the material, cut, metal jewellery, and ornamentation of the upper garments she wore. The garments worn also showed that the wearer was taking part in a ritual or custom. The costumes worn on such occasions usually had certain archaic features, preserved by the strict rules

210
Embroidery on the sleeves and hem of a woman's chemise. Sandanski region. Late 19th century.

211

211
Young men in festive summer costumes. Petrich region. Early 20th century.

which governed the ritual, such as elements of clothing worn in the past and used only on such occasions.

There are no special features about the costumes worn in the performance of customs and rituals connected with work, because these costumes were chiefly adapted to work. Nevertheless, on such occasions certain special accessories were worn with them, and the various garments were worn in different ways. For instance, on St. Tryphon's Day, the 'King of the Vineyards' wears a wreath on his head and on his shoulders. Carol singers (koledari) in Elhovo region carried nosegays decorated with beads and paillettes. One of the members of a group of *koledari* in Sofia region dressed up as a young bride, even wearing the large headdress of artificial flowers and coins. The beauty of the old costumes for women stands out particularly well when the Lazarus Day dances are danced. Girls wear their loveliest clothes on that day, and also accessories and ornaments which are strikingly decorative.

The headdresses worn by the *Lazarki* of Sofia region are particularly distinctive: a *kossichnik* (head ornament) made of flowers, a metal forehead ornament. other ornaments which cover the ears, a bunch of wheat on the head and tinkling necklaces, belt buckles and belts. The *lazarki* of Sliven and Yambol regions place special hats on their heads, which revive old forms, with high cylindrical or shovel-shaped pads covered with artificial flowers and

212

metal jewellery. The costume worn by *lazarki* in the village of Pirin near Sandanski, consists of white *sayas,* richly embroidered chemises, finely ornamented aprons, silver jewellery and many handkerchiefs tucked into the waistband. The person chosen to be the *bouyenets* (leader in the spring dance) adds ornaments and accessories to her costume. The old Slav men's costume, with its long shirt, is worn when dancing as *roussalii* in another ritual, and a distinctive feature of the participation in this custom is the wreath of herbs on their hats and the little bells tied to their sandals. Wedding costumes are most interesting in this respect.

Some of the essential features in a traditional Bulgarian wedding (which is markedly social in character, taking on the form of a folk drama with the aspect of a ritual) are to be found in the costumes,

212
Young woman's summer costume. Gotsedelchev region. Late 19th century.

213

213

Women's summer costumes. Razlog region. Early 20th century.

besides numerous other varied elements and manifestations. Wedding costumes are not worn merely to show the temporary participation of persons in the wedding ritual, they play the part of social signs which show that many of the people attending it belong to a definite social group; they also show their place and situation in the social system. During the wedding ceremony when new and varied social relations are established - between individuals and the family, between the family and the clan-family group and the local inhabitants – as a materialized expression of these relations, the costumes take on the part of their definers and regulators. A wedding is one of the family customs of traditional Bulgarian festivities in which the social function of clothing predominates and fully excludes from people's awareness one of its primary purposes. In both its manifestations this function, a social-differentiating and social-integrating one, is apparent in the whole cycle of rituals and customs accompanying the wedding in its three principal parts: before, during and after the wedding. The social function of clothing during the wedding festivities is particularly striking. It should, however, be noted that this does not affect the essence of the costumes. Wedding costumes keep their character as a type of working clothes adapted to labour conditions and the local population's way of life in the material and cut of the separate garments, in the basic elements and complete compostion, even in the main artistic features and disposition of the ornamentation; this applies chiefly to the villages and also to the towns in part, where farming and stockbreeding predominate, and to a lesser extent the crafts. This also applies chiefly to the outer forms and decoration of the costumes and the elements which make them up in certain cases.

The social function of clothing during a wedding is manifested most strongly and with the greatest effect in the costumes of the bridal couple, the principal actors in the wedding drama. However, it is the bride's costume which holds pride of place, not only because a woman's costume is more sensitive to social relations and undergoes frequent and varied changes, but chiefly because the bride is entering on new social relations. Her clothing takes on this function as soon as a girl becomes of marriageable age and is most often shown in an increase in its dimensions, the established subject now treated in its decoration, the variety of colours used in it, particularly in the most important parts of the costume; this is done by the symbolism of the colours, for instance, the considerable size of the white area on the apron; the definite way in which upper garments and accessories are worn, which enhance the festive character of the costumes in form and outline and increase the area to be decorated; the form of the hair-do, which emphasizes the impression of long, thick hair, one of the elements of the ideal of feminine beauty among the Bulgarians; the constant presence of a bunch of fresh flowers on the head, replaced by a wreath on feast days; supplementary accessories, such as an ornamental handkerchief tucked into the folds of the waistband.

The bridegroom's age is indicated by fewer and more modest elements: richer linear ornamentation of his upper garment; the ornamentation and bright colours of his waistband supplemented by a decorated or woven belt; the way he wears his fur hat, and his footwear – the white puttees with their black woollen strings and the leather sandals, all of which show strength, masculinity and freedom.

Some of the elements of the costumes worn by young people, such as their nosegays, wreaths and handkerchiefs were used to show feelings, even going so far as to hint at proposals. For instance, if a giri gave a young man her nosegay, or if a young man took the girl's nosegay, this was considered as an expression of feeling, in the period when they showed liking for one another; stealing a wreath or a napkin, particularly at the chain dance, was considered as an offer of marriage.

The respective signs on their clothing were not considered sufficient proof of the young people's preparedness for marriage. Since the domestic manner of production was predominant, most of these signs were considered as proof of the industriousness of those who wore them. A girl's maturity was recognized when em-

214

214
Apron from Gotsedelchev region. Late19th century.

broideries and weaves on her clothes, with patterns showing her age, but usually difficult to achieve, appeared on her clothes; they usually required skill, patience and even a creative spirit, all qualities desirable in a young married woman. After successfully undergoing tests as a farmer and householder, tests which usually took place when he was first allowed to plough on his own, a young man was allowed to change his boyhood garments for those of a bachelor; this indicated that he was admitted to the circles of adult men.

The transition of persons from one stage in their family status to another, marked by the period of engagement, was evidenced by a combination of elements in the respective costumes of women and brides, and of bachelors and bridegrooms. When a girl got engaged, the costume she wore was brightended by the jewellery she was given by her fiancé and his family. Her fiancé's festive costume was enhanced by the 'golden nosegay', made up of certain definite garden flowers, decorated with gold pieces, and by the handkerchief, embroidered by his fiancée, which he tucked into his waistband.

As the supreme moment in the cycle of wedding rituals and customs approached, the circle of wedding personages was extended and costumes differentiated in various ways, particularly by their artistic form, came to the fore. Persons who played a part in the wedding ritual showed this in their costumes. The bride's costume was strikingly differentiated. She wore a large number of garments which were beautifully ornamented, and also had special accessories. In many parts of the country, particularly in the South, the principal garments of a regular woman's costume (chemise, *soukman,* apron, etc.) were doubled at the wedding; in other parts of the country a waistband and belt was added to it. In certain regions – Thrace and the Pirin region – a 'red chemise' was even prepared; it was usually an ordinary chemise of white fabric, but with its visible parts, such as sleeves and skirts, made of red silk material. The wearing of certain garments, such as an outer garment usually made of white woollen fabric, was taboo for girls, but obligatory for a bride. The head cover, the most strikingly distinctive feature of a bride's costume, had to be red, and large enough to cover the head and drop down over the face.; it was rarely yellow, and only in more recent times was it white. This bridal cover was usually worn with wreaths and ornaments of very varied form, from an ordinary wreath to a small cylindrical basket, and a semicircular ornament with a diameter up to 50-60 cm, as in Sofia region. The napkin which covered her hands was an obligatory accessory to the bride's costume during the wedding ceremonies.

This costume was differentiated not so much by the quantity and effect of its ornamentation, as by the designs, chiefly on the principal garment, the chemise, which had more ornamentation on it than any other part of the costume. For instance, in some parts of the Danubian Plain a bird's figure, called *kachoulan* (Roussé district) was the main feature of the design; a zig-zag fiery red line known as 'dragons' heads' (Pleven district); in some villages of the Pirin region, the embroidered skirts of a bride's chemise were said to be 'blackened', because of the black contour around the

215 216.
Apron from Sandanski region. Late 19th century.

215

216

217
Young woman's costume Kurdjali region. Early 20th century.

218
Men's and women's costumes from Kurdjali region. Late 19th century.

pattern, explained as symbolizing the bride's grief at losing her youth and leaving her father's home, while in other villages the embroidered stripe had some large motifs on the back of the skirt. This differentiation of the bridal garments as far as their ornamentation went was even apparent in the various names they were given, because they were worn in the period when the bride was supposed to be silent in the presence of her new relations, and to bow to them at all times.

The costume of the bridegroom was less open to expressing social relations, as was apparent in the description of men's costumes in general; he only had to wear a long outer garment or sheepskin jacket, belts or napkins crossed over his chest, and a towel wound around his neck; a nosegay of garden flowers, and feathers on his fur hat; only in some parts of Western Bulgaria was his face covered with a white handkerchief.

The external effect of distinctive signs on the costumes of the wedding guests gradually grew less according to their place in the wedding procession, and depended on their role in the rituals and customs.

After the costumes of bride and bridegroom, next in importance came those of the bridegroom's brother and sister, who took part in almost all the rituals and customs, from the invitation to the wedding to unveiling the bride. For the brother-in-law, the difference in his wedding garb from his ordinary festive clothes was that he had more accessorries, and ornamented his fur hat with feathers, wreaths of flowers, twigs, dried fruit and even vegetables; he also had belts and towels crossed over his breast, and sometimes he even tied on the shirt his new sister-in-law had given him. The sister-in-law's role in the wedding ceremony

217

218

219

affected one of the basic parts of her costume, in which very old elements were often found, for instance, as regards colour: the outer garment was made of undyed fabrics, and she wore more clothes – an outer garment, usually made of a red fabric, red or white handkerchiefs, crossed across her breast etc. At many places the eldest sister-in law dressed in some of the bride's garments; this was a relic of elements in rituals connected with a girl's entering upon the marriageable age.

Insignificant signs were worn by wedding guests related to the bride or bridegroom, according to the part they played in the rituals and customs – the flowers of which their wreaths were made, the nosegays on the fur hats and garments, the way in which they carried their gifts.

When the climax in the wedding ceremony was reached – the actual exchange of rings, together with the customs aimed at

219
Young woman's festive costume. Kurdjali region. Early 20th century.

220

Women's head scarves (back view). Haskovo region. Early 20th century.

221

Girl's festive costume. Haskovo region. Early 20th century,

220

221

222

bringing the bride into the circle of the family and the women as a new member, the social-differentiating functions of the costumes yielded to the the social-integrating functions.

222 Young women in summer festive costumes. Haskovo region. Early 20th century.

The traditional Bulgarian national wedding costumes marked the height of artistic achievements and the people's skill as modellers.The entire aesthetic function of these costumes sheds light on essential features of the Bulgarian people's mentality, according to which beauty must make its way into all spheres of life and labour and ways of living. In folk poetry the *ethic role* of aesthetic functions of clothing is expressed: bright and joyous feelings are aroused in people at the sight of a girl or a bride, dressed in their costumes, shaped by the laws of beauty. Beautiful clothing, as an expression of the wonderful, is combined with a sense of nobility. The revolutionary's request for a 'white shirt' and well-combed hair persistently shows this link between the aesthetic function of clothing and the ethics of social relations.

The beginnings, development and links of Bulgarian national costumes with all sides of the people's life form an unwritten history of the population which wore them, showing their cultural and historical relations at various epochs, indicating their economic and social development, their artistic gifts and skilful implementation. Because of the place they occupy as one of the essential parts of Bulgarian national culture, Bulgarian national costumes deserve to be brought forward as one of the most striking means of expressing their national specifics.

223
Girls dressed as *Lazarki.* Sandanski region. Early 20th century.

224 225
Needle-point lace on the front opening and sleeve of a woman's chemise. Second half of 19th century from Koprivshtitsa

223

224 225

226
Apron and ornamentation of a *soukman* hem. Haskovo region. Early 20th century.

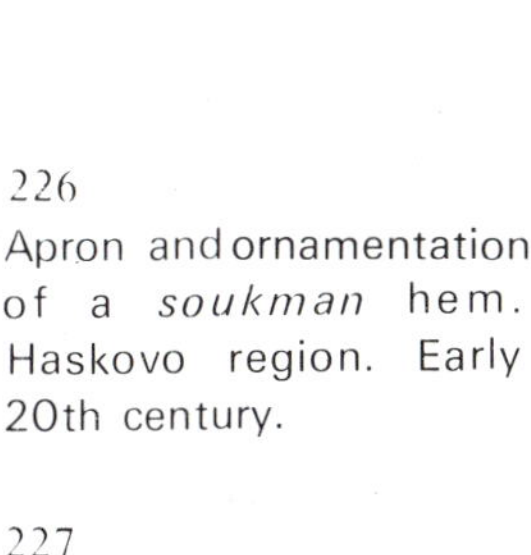

227
Young woman in festive costume, Haskovo district. Early 19th century.

226 227

SNEZHANA
DANCHEVA-BLAGOEVA

BULGARIAN FOLK

EWELLERY

BULGARIAN FOLK JEWELLERY

Jewellery made of metal was worn with Bulgarian national costumes. Like the traditional garments, they performed certain functions in the people's life, but their uniqueness was due to the fact that they had a definite significance, since, compared with the garments, their practical usefulness was far less.

Jewellery travelled a long and complex road until it reached its present decorative purpose. This road was closely connected with the development of man's material and cultural life, with his world outlook, mentality and aesthetic requirements at various epochs. Much of the jewellery developed from certain articles which served a practical purpose in joining separate garments. The first jewellery with which man adorned himself was made of seeds, flowers, shells, the teeth of slain animals, etc. At a later date, when metals had been discovered, it was made by certain people who were technically more experienced and had shown artistic talent. In the eyes of primitive man, jewellery, particularly when made of metal, possessed magical protective power. We know that most of it was placed at the most vulnerable parts of the human body. Our forefathers were unaware of the properties of destroying microbes possessed by metals, properties already proved by chemistry and biology today. Gold and silver were particularly strong bactericides, but together with these properties, as Marx put it, 'they were virgin light,dug out of the underground world, silver reflecting all the rays in their initial mixing while gold - only the strongest colour - red.But a sense of colour is the most popular form of aesthetic feeling in general.... Their aesthetic properties made them a virgin material for luxury, decoration, brilliance, festive use, in short – a positive form of abundance and wealth.''

In Antiquity certain pieces of jewellery were used as military dis-

1

2

1
Ear-covers, Western Bulgaria, 10th-14th century. Silver, silver alloy, gilding.

2
Ear-covers, Western Bulgaria, 14th-16th century.

tinctions. They showed remarkable vitality, and their forms and decoration crystallized in many ritual jewels, used in the head-dresses of brides even in more recent times.

The cultures of many peoples, who inhabited our lands at various times, have left an imprint on the aspect of traditional Bulgarian jewellery. When they settled in the Balkan Peninsula the Slavs and the Proto-Bulgarians found a rich cultural heritage, left by the Thracians, the Hellenes, the Romans and the Byzantines. The gold earrings, fibulae, pectorals, ornaments for cuirasses, and gold bracelets weighing up to 450 gr worn by the Thracians, were very different from the exquisite forms of the Greek ornaments. Thracian jewellery was closer to that of the Scythians, but was distinguished from it by its original artistic style. The Thracian goldsmiths did filigree work, along with the basic techniques of their craft, casting and embossing, as early as the 5th to 4th century.

The Slavs brought to our lands their ornaments for the head, torques, fibulae, bracelets, buttons, pendentives and amulets, made chiefly of silver, copper and bronze. Some of the Slav ear-covers were also marks of tribal and territorial affiliation. In the 5th century A. D. Slav goldsmiths were masters of one of the most difficult techniques – filigree work in silver or copper wire. Triangles, circles, rows of embossed or concave dots were typical Slav decorations. The design of a circlet with a dot in the middle, familiar to us from the Hallstatt epoch, was the magical symbol of an eye for them, which guarded the owner from the evil eye, or of a solar sign, which brought luck. In Slav ornaments images of horses were used, probably connected with the idea of the sun and bearers of happiness, prosperity and good fortune. Images of birds were symbols of fertility.

3

3
Ear-covers, Western Bulgaria, 16th-17th century.

4

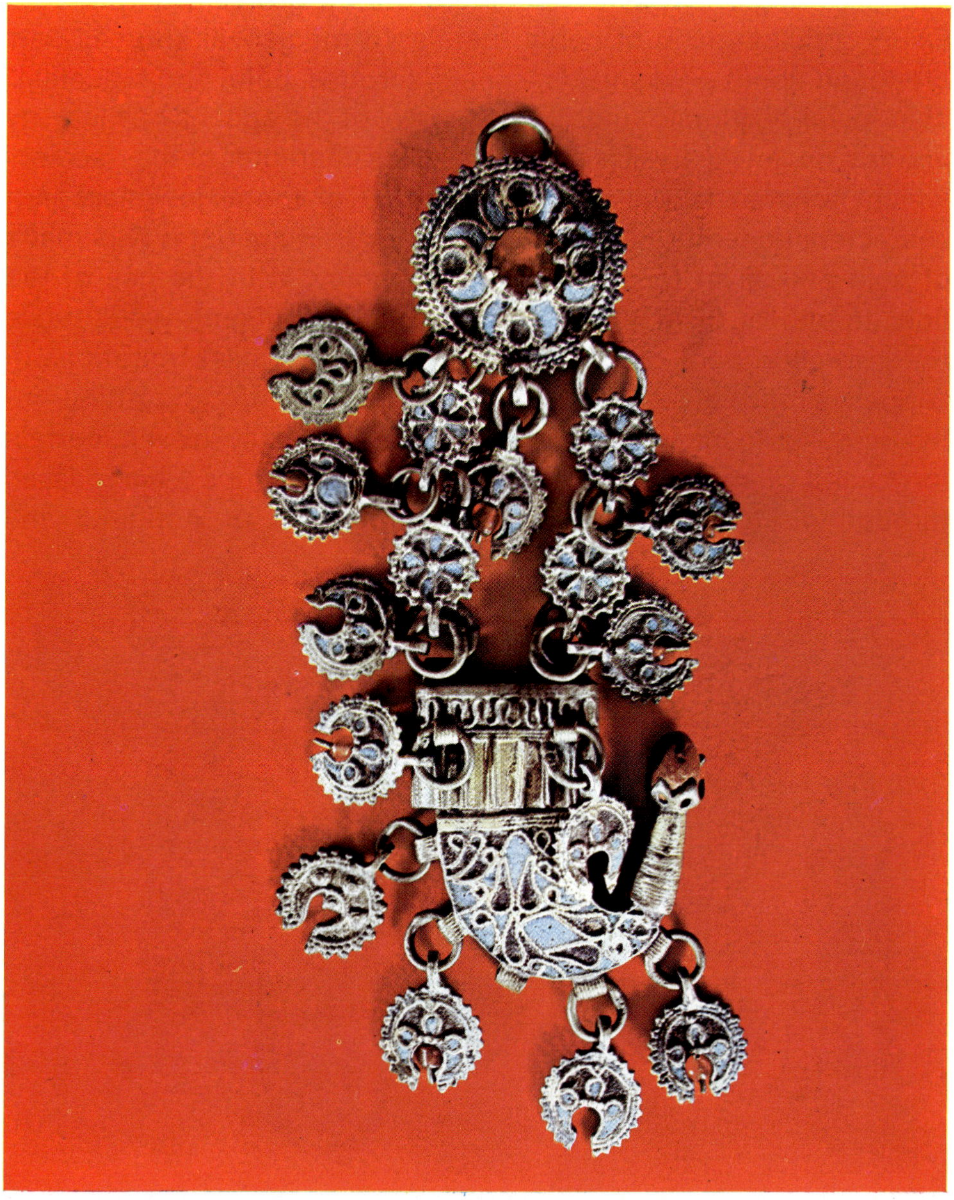

4
Claw ear-pendant from Samokov region, 18th-19th century

The Proto-Bulgarians wore leather belts studded with bronze, silver or gold ornaments. They were usually open work ornaments, and some of the gold belt ornaments were worked in filigree in the 7th to 8th centuries, borders, and triangular and diamond-shaped decorative motifs of granules being welded onto them, and also motifs made of gold wire. Proto-Bulgarian jewellery had the polychromatic quality of certain decorative principles found in Eastern art, with which they had been in contact before settling in the Balkan Peninsula. Small flat pieces of quartz in various colours and enamel were used as additional decoration. Metal belt ornaments probably had a magical purpose and played the part of amulets. Perhaps that was why the Proto-Bulgarians did not wear special amulets, as the Slavs did, but this Slav tradition was preserved in the newly-founded Slav-Bulgarian State. Among the 8th and 9th century amulets, which have come down to us, there are some in the form of axes, bows and arrows, birds, horses' heads or dogs. In this period there was a growing demand for luxury articles made of noble metals. In mediaeval sources data are found about gold shields, spears, torques, belts and bracelets. The social-economic and cultural level of the epochs has left its imprint on jewellery. It shows the class character of the society which fathered it. The class distribution of metal jewellery is a characteristic feature of the Middle Ages in Bulgaria: it was made of gold and silver for the feudal aristocracy, with the use of the finer toreutical techniques of embossing and filigree work, while the jewellery worn by the people consisted of cast imitations in copper, bronze or silver alloys. Besides artistic Byzantine influences, Bulgarian mediaeval jewellery also borrowed certain forms and ornaments from the various ethnic groups which passed through our country. The artistic traditions of Antiquity and

5
Ear-pendants with *pod-bradnik,* South-Western Bulgaria, 19th century

6
Ear ornaments with *pod-bradnik,* Western Bulgaria, 14-th-16th century

7
Ear-pendants with *pod-bradnik,* South-Western Bulgaria, 19th century

5

6

7

Byzantine influences were more strongly apparent in works intended for the ruling class. The Slav and partly the Proto-Bulgarian tradition was preserved and developed in the folk jewellery. The nobility first adopted the fashionable influences coming from abroad, while the people kept to their own artistic culture with its specific ethnical features for a long time.

Much of the mediaeval Bulgarian jewellery which has come down to us has the features of a highly specialized goldsmiths' art. Various techniques have been used in making this jewellery, such as casting, wrought work and embossing, engraving, openwork, filigree enamel work, the setting of precious and semi-precious stones and glass, etc.

The Ottoman invasion did severe and lasting damage to the whole of Bulgarian art. In the first centuries of bondage the production of jewellery on a large scale was drastically reduced because the peasants who bought it had lost their purchasing power. In some of the centres of this craft, particularly in the Western Bulgarian lands, certain traditions in the making of ear-covers, bracelets, rings, etc., were preserved to a certain extent.

Foreign travellers who visited the Bulgarian lands during the first centuries of bondage noted the great weakness the women had for decking themselves out with metal jewellery. According to data provided by recent researches, in this period most of the peasants in the villages met their own needs, as far as jewellery was concerned, and did not depend on the goldsmiths. 'In view of the generally increased cost of living in the Balkan domains of the Ottoman Empire in the 16th and 17th centuries, in most regions the Bulgarian peasant women were forced to replace the expensive metal jewellery made by craftsmen by local Turkish and West European coins which were in circulation in large quantities

8

8
Arpalii earrings, Vidin region, 19th century

9

10

at greatly reduced values and served the Balkan markets at that time.' In this period the women themselves made their bridal hats, breast ornaments, *kossichnicks,* the *podbradnitsi* and necklaces made of silver coins threaded together or sewn onto cloth. Although it was chiefly the rich brides who decked themselves in this way, coins were used mainly because of their metal and their essential function was one of magical protection. There was a widespread belief that in times of epidemics all the metal jewellery they possessed had to be worn by the women, and a gold or a silver coin had to be kept in the mouth.

In the 18th century jewellery made by goldsmiths gradually began to spread amid wider circles of the population, displacing the home-made decoration of coins to a certain extent. This was not a regular process in all parts of the country. It was characteristic of the regions which were developing more rapidly economically.

During the period of Ottoman bondage oriental ornaments, with the numerous chains and pendants characteristic of them which tinkled at every movement, had a prolonged and lasting influence on Bulgarian jewellery. This oriental influence in ornamentation was apparent in the adoption of certain decorative elements characteristic of the East, such as the late Turkish arabesque, a pointed and broken arch, the half-moon, elements of the ' tulip style, etc.

Already during the first centuries of bondage, craftsmen in the old

9
Ear-covers with *podbradnik,* Panagyurishté region, 18th-19th century

10
Ear pendants with *kaburi-* type *podbradnik,* Topolvgrad region, 19th century

11

11
Trepka, Western Bulgaria, 18th-19th century

mediaeval Bulgarian centres of the goldsmiths' art continued and further developed the old mediaeval tradition of *cloisonné* enamel, along with the basic techniques of casting, embossing and filigree work; *cloisonné* enamel work at this time also underwent the favourable influence of the goldsmiths of Dubrovnik. The variant in which the cells were formed by twisted or flat wire was widespread. The goldsmiths used the original technique of *cloisonné* enamel to decorate their more expensive and artistic work made of silver and gilding, and principally intended for the church and partly for the rich Turkish and Bulgarian notables. The craftsmen's jewellery made in the 18th century and intended for wider distribution was cast from bronze or cheap silver alloys. Instead of enamel, various coloured clays and glazes were used, and in the better grades of silver alloys – glass beads, pounded to dust, were used. Various ornaments for the head were made in imitation of *cloisonné* enamel at this time, such as *trepki* (ear-covers), pendents worn over the ears, pendants which ornamented the *kossichniks* (ornamental covers for the hair), necklaces, rings, belts and belt buckles. In casting, forms and motifs already made were used, and sometimes whole pieces of jewellery, embossed or worked in filigree. Some of the details of the design on cast articles were sometimes additionally embossed or hammered.
From about the end of the 18th century, the craftsmen in the centres of the goldsmiths' craft of economically more highly

developed regions began to use with increasing frequency the technique of wrought metal work and openwork filigree in the production of the traditional folk jewellery, which was growing in scale. It is known that these two techniques in toreutics require the use of purer silver alloys, also making possible the use of templets in production at a higher artistic level.

The goldsmiths used punches, called *kalemi* in making the design in relief. The contours of the design were first outlined with a point or a pencil. The articles were embossed on both sides on a mixture of resin. The basic outlines of the relief were shaped from the lower side with the help of a more rounded *kalem.* The exact artistic modelling was done after the work was turned with the right side outward, and finer *kalemi* were used to shape the embossed details of the ornamental design. Some of the jewellery ornamented by embossing shows that many of the goldsmiths of the National Revival period were artists in their craft and were able to sculpt. Some of the *kalemi* used in embossing were matrices of small decorative elements: rosettes, buds, grains, small lines and small crosses. A certain mechanization of production was obtained by the use of metal templets, made of bronze or iron. They were called matrices or *baskii*. When the templet was struck with a hammer it sank into the metal and the desired ornament was obtained. That is how earrings, *tepeluks* (head pins) and bracelets were embossed. In some cases matrices were used to outline only the general contours of the ornaments from the underside, and then it was hammered again from the upper side with *kalemi.* In this way the preliminary work of drawing and hammering the ornament on the under side was avoided, while the modelling on the upper side with *kalemi* offered a certain possibility for creative work to every craftsman, even though

12

Trepka, Skankédimitrov region, 19th century

13

Bride's nosegay, South-Western Bulgarian, Pirin region, 19th century

12

13

within the framework of a given templet. Each individual piece of jewellery thus bore its own individuality and beauty. This manner of embossing was particularly characteristic in shaping ornaments in relief on buckles in the goldsmiths' National Revival centres, such as Panagyurishté, Karlovo, Pazardjik, Plovdiv and Kotel.

Pressing with matrices was done by means of cast matrices – positive and negative. The piece of wrought metal was placed between them and they were placed in a vice which was tightened, or hammered, until the piece of metal had acquired the form of the matrix.

Rings and the narrow pieces of metal for bracelets were wrought on special anvils on which there were grooves with various patterns.

Some of the loveliest, but nevertheless comparatively widespread jewellery of the National Revival period was made of pure silver, gilded and worked in openwork filigree. It sometimes formed alone the framework of the articles, while at other times the openwork filigree surfaces were appliquéd on cast, or smoothly wrought platelets. The separate filigree elements were shaped in iron templet frames. The material with which this technique was worked, drawn wires, determined the character and structure of the filigree ornament. Although this material offered greater possibilities for a linear treatment of the ornament the National Revival goldsmiths also created forms in volume by embossing the linearly formed rosettes. Together with certain other plant elements worked in this way, these forms were placed upon the flatly made filigree curves on the surfaces of the articles. In this way movement was given to the filigree composition and the artistic effect was enhanced. The beautifully worked filigree curves, the small metal balls and diamond-shaped metal pieces, the small

14
Bride's nosegay, Pirin region, 19th century

14

15

15
Head ornament, South-Western Bulgaria, 19th century

flowers which blossomed on the airy lace-like designs brought a joyous element to the filigree compositions of the National Revival period. The granular technique which ornamented the surface of articles with thickly welded silver or gold grains, was chiefly used in forming the balls of the big head pins.

The goldsmiths of the National Revival period also made openwork ornaments by casting and embossing. The cast openwork was made by first making openwork models, and in the case of embossed ornamental designs by cutting away the background. Openwork cut out decorative surfaces were sometimes rivetted onto the smooth cast plates of buckles. These decorative surfaces were sometimes gilded. The contrast between the silver of the foundation and the gold of the openwork gave movement and suppleness to the ornamental composition.

The goldmiths of the National Revival period gradually began to rid themselves of the geometrical and schematic style of mediaeval toreutics prevalent during the first centuries of bondage, and also of certain oriental motifs in ornamentation. The jewellery of this period shows a joyous and energetic mood. Certain older traditions in the use of palmettes and roses continued to be used and further developed as decorative elements. Palmettes were often broken up and reworked as trefoils, lilies and semi-palmettes. The goldsmiths of this period used certain very old plant forms as ornaments, such as cypresses, vines and acanthus leaves. The mediaeval manner of flat and schematic treatment of acanthus leaves was abandoned. They now covered National Revival jewellery with an abundance of leaves that made for a happy mood.

New elements made their way into National Revival forms and ornaments; they were borrowed from West European decorative

16
Prochelnik of the *stefan* type, Preslav region, 19th century

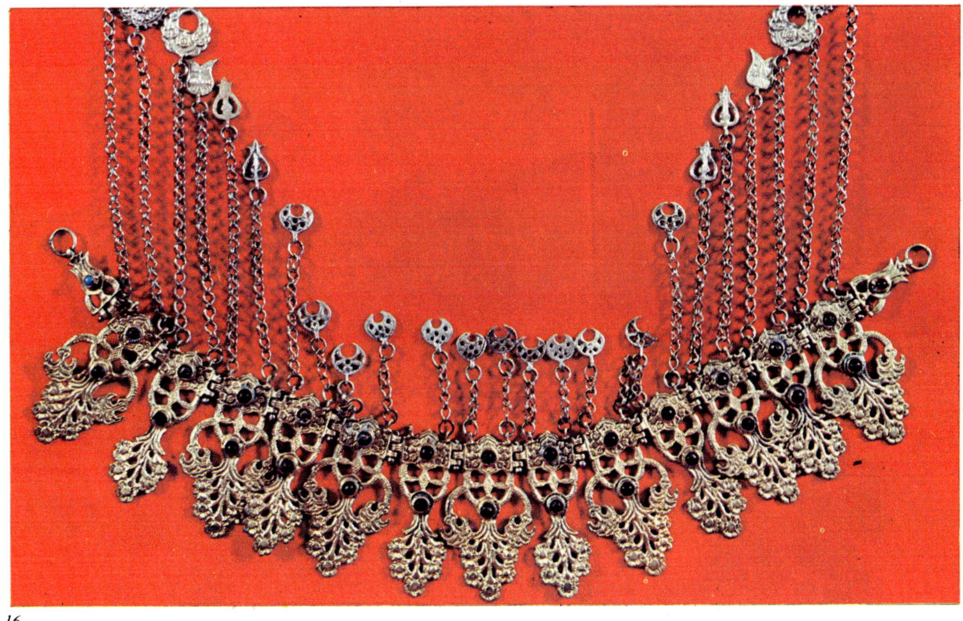

16

17
Himaïl ornament for the head, Haskovo region, 19th century

17

18
Prochelnik of the *stefan* type Preslav region, 19th century

18

19

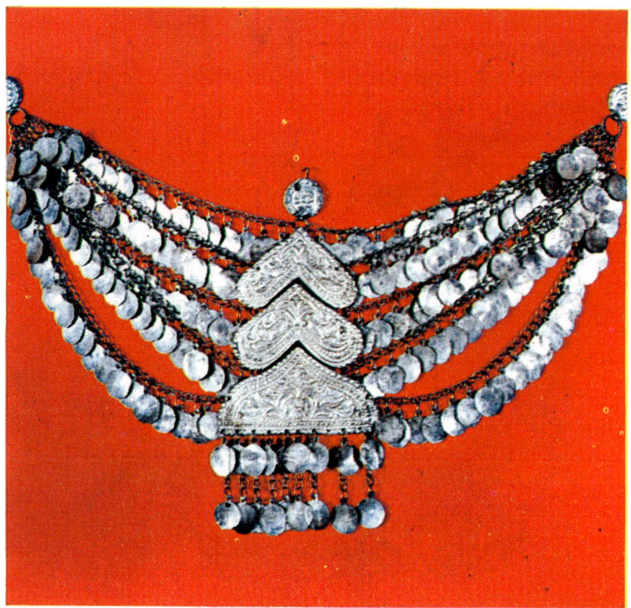

20

styles: Renaissance, Baroque, Rococo and Empire. The Eastern influences, which had very old traditions in our country, were enriched in this period by a number of new forms and subjects, such as compositions of poplars, strawberries, rose twigs, human personifications of the sun, and ornaments of an arabesque character. Local traditions and the creative possibilities of the Bulgarian goldsmiths made it possible to adapt these borrowings to the artistic requirements of the Bulgarians in this epoch. In ornamentation foreign decorative motifs were reduced to such as were the closest to the local flora and fauna.

Plant ornaments composed of flowers, twigs and garlands of flowers embossed in low or higher relief sometimes occupied the whole surface of the jewellery. Ornamental plant motifs were treated in many different ways: from a naturalistic interpretation to stylization which sometimes passed into ornament. Geometrical ornaments were usually used in making borders, and consisted mostly of dots, slanting incised lines, festooning and meandering lines. Figural ornamentation also had its place in National Revival jewellery. The human figure was found in compositions of a religious character on belt buckles. The images of birds and other animals were usually placed in the centre of the decorative composition. Archtitectural silhouettes were always extremely conventional.

In spite of external influences the National Revival jewellery shows original artistic features and the perfect skill of the goldsmiths of this period.

19
Circlet of the *sokai* head-dress, Gabrovo region, 19th century

20
Prochelnik, Haskovo region, 19th century

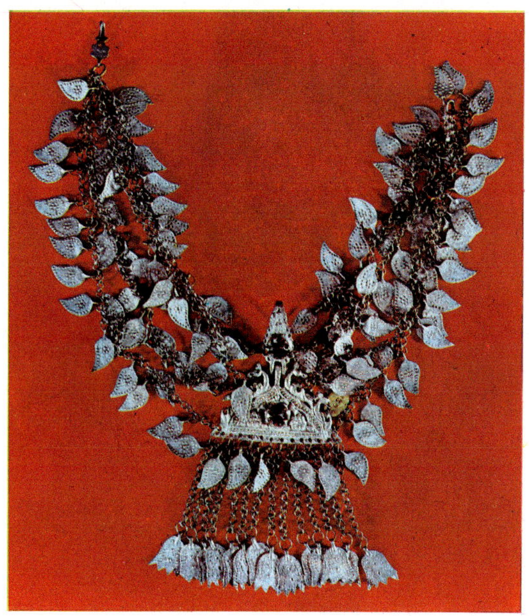

21

22

21
Prochelnik, Samokov region, 19th century

22
Prochelnik, South-Western Bulgaria, 19th century

It is difficult to cover the great variety of Bulgarian folk jewellery of the last few centuries, about which ethnographic research on the terrain is still to be carried out. The development of jewellery in this period went hand in hand with the formation and development of Bulgarian national costumes.
According to the part of the body on which it was worn, jewellery can be divided into two basic groups: jewellery ornamenting the head and jewellery ornamenting the body.
Jewellery worn on the head together with the intricate ways of arranging the head scarf have very old elements and regional distinctions. Ear-covers and earrings are an old Slav form of ornamentation. The bulb-shaped earrings and ear-covers were widely accepted by women in the Slav-Bulgarian State which had come into being. The ear-covers were made of silver, silver alloys, gold, copper or bronze. In the Middle Ages and in more recent times they were worn by women of all classes and strata of Bulgarian society. In the mediaeval necropolises earrings and ear-covers were found in pairs or alone, and sometimes as many as five on both sides of the skull. The ear-covers were usually attached to the head dress, or braided into the hair, while the earrings were thrust through holes, pierced for the purpose in the lobes.
Ear-covers were usually round. The old smooth or twisted hoop gradually grew more complicated and was ornamented with small rings and spherical forms composed of grains, prismatic, biconical or bipyramidal ornaments.
In the 13th and 14th centuries the women of the feudal nobility wore two new types of ear-covers. The first of these was based on a large, round hollow body with an indentation at its upper end, and a semi-circular hoop by which it was attached. Some of this type of ear-covers which have come down to us show great

technical and artistic skill. Elements of openwork filigree were used in decorating them, and this was a comparatively difficult technique to use in the Middle Ages. Sometimes these jewels were linked with a *podbradnik* (under-chin ornament) made of braided wire. They were very close in form to the jewellery depicted on the hat worn by Dessislava in the fresco of Boyana Church (dated 1259). The second type of these luxurious jewels was like a small wreath of flowers. They were semi-circular in form and consisted of a hollow body curved in the shape of an arc, to which little cone-shaped tubes and a small round hoop were radially attached. Square transparent stones, placed in high metal settings, were used as additional decoration. Ear-covers of this kind were found in Bulgaria at the village of Dragizhevo and are dated to the 14th century. Both types of ear-covers are to be seen on many portraits of Bulgarian and Serbian *Tsaritsas and boyarkas.* They were obviously a characteristic part of their head ornaments. They were attached to the hats or to the diadems by pearl chains.The Russian *kolti* are similar to them; they were worn by the Russian *boyarkas.* Little pieces of cloth, imbued with aromatic substances, were found in some of the hollow mediaeval ear-covers.

Ear-covers and earrings continued to be worn during the period of Ottoman bondage. During the first centuries of bondage the craftsmen's traditions of making these jewels was localized chiefly in the Westen Bulgarian lands. In other parts of the country these jewels were made by hand from coins by the Bulgarian women. From about the 18th century ear-covers made by craftsmen became more widespread. In this period, under oriental influences, little chains with pendents which tinkled were added

23
Detail of a *chomoloushka* head pin

24
Chomoloushka head pin, Western Bulgaria, 18th-19th century

25
Detail of a *chomoloushka* head pin

23

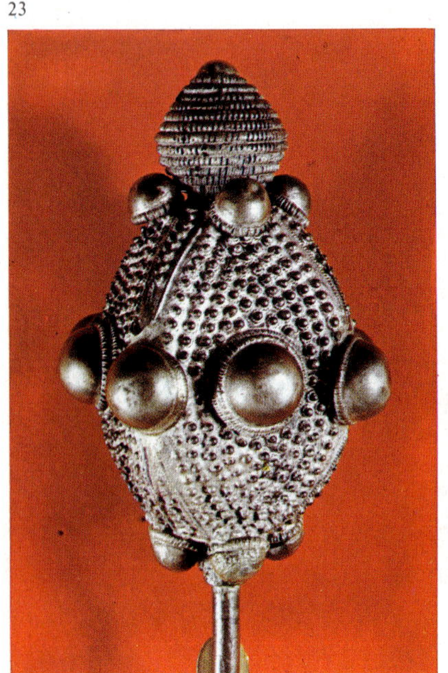

24

25

to certain old local forms. A characteristic form for the ear-covers made in the Western Bulgarian lands was a thin ornamented plaque like a half-moon attached to the lower half of a large round hoop, with a fastening. Other ear-covers, also made under oriental influence, have as their foundation a semicircular, flat and hollow body. The surface was decorated with granulation, obtained by embossing. There was a large round hoop on the upper part and cast decorative pendants were attached to its lower part by small rings.

Ear-covers made in the form of a claw, from which they took their name, are of special interest. These were hung over the temples and consisted of two platelets, ornamented with *cloisonné* enamel, or its cast imitations, and also with glass stones. The lower platelet was like a box and was shaped like a bird's claw. It had a small lid and various herbs were placed in it, or other objects which served as amulets. This piece of jewellery was clearly an amulet, since it was believed that, as they served to defend birds and animals, claws would inspire fear, and divert evil looks, preserving from evil forces and the evil eye whoever wore their symbols.

Ear-covers, made of platelets set with carnelians or other coloured semi-precious stones or glass, arranged in free perpendicular rows, with freely hanging small chains on which there were decorative pendants, were particularly handsome. They were often linked by a common longer chain which passed under the head like a *podbradnik.*

At some places the ear-covers were of the type of the many-branched pendants like the "little snakes" of the sokai head-

26
Head pin, Western Bulgaria, 18th-19th century

27
Head pin, Toutrakan region, 19th century

28
Head pin, Razgrad region, 19th century

26

27

28

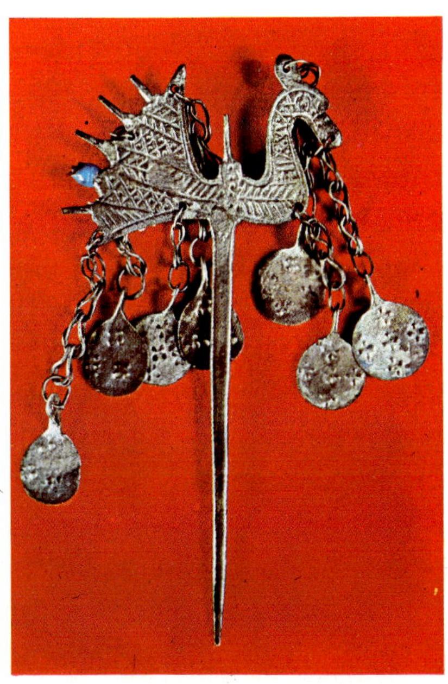

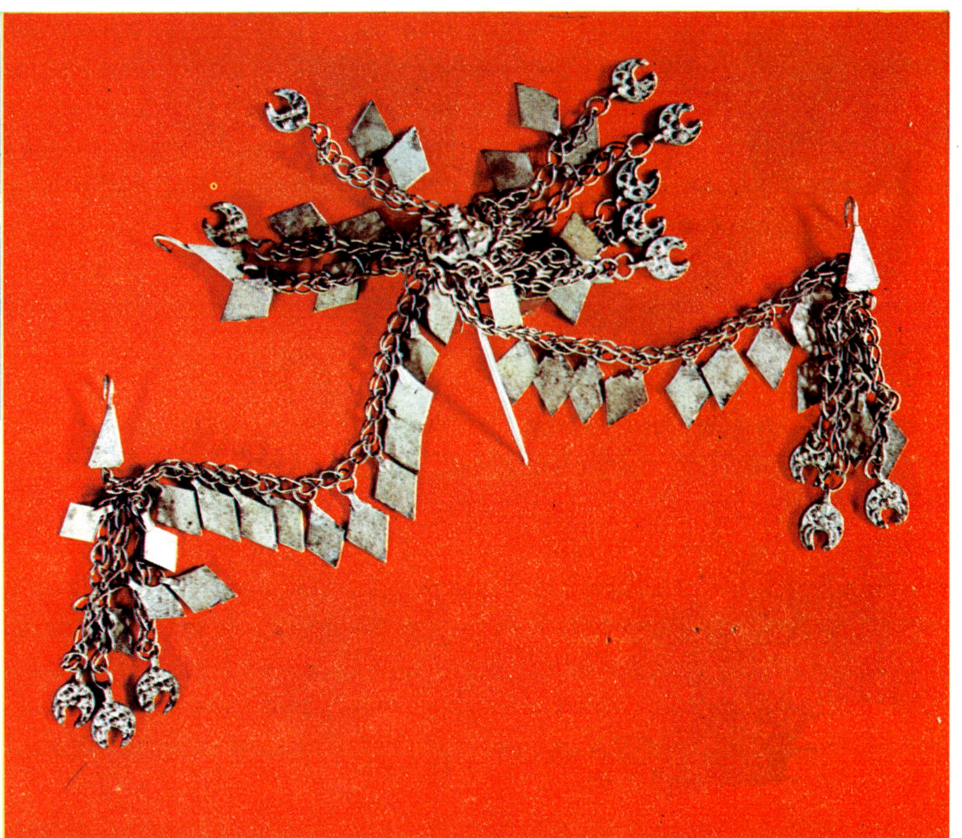

29

dress. They consisted of one or two cast triangular platelets with separated cast rosettes appliquéd on them. Their surfaces were decorated with stylized plant ornaments. Glass stones, placed in special nests, were used as additional decoration. Small chains, to which were attached plain or openwork cast flower-like decorative pendants or round sections hung from the lower edge of the platelets.

29
Head pin, Yambol region, 19th century

In the Thracian Lowlands *kaburi* ('tintacks') were worn. An oblong pear-shaped body formed the basis of their cast foundation; they were close in form to the mediaeval ear-covers worn in this region. The *kaburi* had long chains hanging from their lower edge, decorated with cast or cut-out decorative pendants. Some of these ear-covers were connected by a longer chain, which passed under the chin like a *podbradnik.*

In more recent times these heavy and unpractical ear-covers were displaced by various artistically made earrings. There was much finesse and exquisite workmanship in them. In the 19th century, earrings called *arpalii* were widespread in North-Western Bulgaria and later in other parts of the country. These jewels consisted of a circle worked in filigree with an openwork rosette in relief in the centre. Grains were arranged around the circle like small barley grains. At some places these earrings were passed through the ear lobes, but in Chiprovtsi and Berkovitsa they were tied with a thread which passed behind the head. These earrings were an

30
Head pin. North Western Bulgaria, 19th century

30

31
Head pin, Vratsa region, 19th century

31

32

obligatory jewel for every bride. The 'mounts' of gold coins of various sizes gradually developed into independently made earrings of silver or gold. Some of the examples made in the second half of the 19th century show refined artistic taste. Moon-shaped earrings, which have a very old Slav tradition, were also worn in the 19th century. The earrings worn in various parts of the country were very varied in form, decoration and names. In Kotel, for instance, small earrings, called *echoumichentsa* (small barley grains) were worn by small girls; they consisted of a round hoop and a metal grain. Brides and girls who were engaged to be married wore in their ears gold or silver coins, attached to small twised wires which passed through their lobes. In the Sredna Gora region these little wires were ornamented by decoratively wrought platelets, or some were covered with filigree work.

In the period of Ottoman domination women attached to the back of their heads or to their foreheads various ornamented platelets, either pinned or hooked on, and various decorative pendants attached to chains. The quivering of these pendants when walking gave this piece of jewellery its name – *trepka.* In Western Bulgaria the *trepki* were usually round and ornamented with *cloisonné* enamel, the cells of which were made of filigree, or else of cast imitations. Glass or semi-precious stones and gilding were used as additional ornamentation. In other regions of the country, principally the Thracian Lowlands, the *trepki* are made of two cast

32
Head pin, Vidin region, 19th century

33

33
Tepeluk, Provadia region, 17th century

and decorated triangular or rectangular platelets with rounded corners, loosely joined together by small chains on which there were pendants, and which hung freely from the edge of the lower platelet.

In South-Western Bulgaria bridal jewellery was a variant to these jewels. The foundation of this jewellery was a platelet, cast in openwork and additionally embossed in an arc-shaped, or palmette or triangular form, decorated with a stylized plant design and often with two birds. Mercury gilding was used as additional ornamentation and also semi-precious stones or glass. Two little chains with pendants were attached to one or both sides of the platelet, and shorter little chains with small round platelets at their ends hung from the lower edge.The *himaīl* was like the two jewels already described, but it was characteristic of certain bridal headdresses in the Thracian Lowlands in the region of Haskovo. Its foundation was a wrought platelet in a drawn-out arc form with a stylized plant ornament and two little birds on its upper part. Small chains hung freely from its lower edge, with round platelets imitating Turkish coins. They had a hook on each side by which they were attached.

A shining band around the head, on which silver or copper platelets were sewn, was an old Slav headdress for women. It covered the forehead and the back of the head, holding in the hair. Its ends were tied at the back or held by a pin. This was an old Slav headdress for girls, used on solemn occasions. In more recent times, as the crafts developed in the last centuries of Ottoman bondage, the goldsmiths of North-Western Bulgaria produced a wreathfor girlsof silver or copper platelets, cut or cast in a decorative form. It was worn when a girl was already mature, at the turn of the 19th and 20th century it began to be worn only when she got engaged, and in some cases only on her wedding day.

In the regions where the goldsmith's craft was well developed in the National Revival period, the old forehead ornament worn by girls developed into one of the most beautiful of a bride's jewels called *prochelnik,* because it was worn on the forehead *(chelo).* In the regions of Provadiya and Preslav the prochelnik was called a *stefan* (Greek for wreath) and was in the form of a diadem, composed of platelets, usually cast in openwork and representing flowers. Small chains ornamented with pendants were attached to the lower edge. The *prochelnik* or *kruzhila* (circlet) worn with the *sokai* style of wearing the head scarf, was a cast metal semi-circle made of three arcs, joined by hinges; they were ornamented with a cast imitation of filigree wires welded onto them, consisting of rosettes and artificial stones. In Southern Bulgaria, chiefly in the Thracian Lowlands, the *prochelniks* were usually made of one or more platelets, in the shape of triangles, ellipses or arcs, or any other decoratively cut form, hinged together. Long chains with pendants on them were attached to each end. The ends of the chains were hooked together. Shorter chains with pendants, hung from the lower edges of the platelets. Some of the platelets of these ornaments had two symmetrically placed cast and stylized images of birds (Thrace), or horses' heads (Samokov region).

34
Tepeluk, South Bulgaria, 19th century

35
Tepeluk, South Bulgaria, 19th century

34

35

These images were reminiscences of old Slav symbols. Some of the *prochelniks* in South-Western Bulgaria had a round platelet in the middle and palmette shaped side pieces to hide the hooks by which they were attached to the head. They were decorated with a wrought openwork ornament and gilding The little chains had round, ball-like openwork pendants and also diamond-shaped ones with an ornament embossed in relief and gilded.

Artistically worked pins were also used to hold the bride's head scarf in place. Some of the oldest of these which have come down to us were made in the 18th century and were more like skewers than pins. They were 20 cm long, with heads shaped like ovals or pyramids and ornamented with granules. Their surfaces had large semispheres on them, surrounded at the base by decorative wires and were thickly studded with small granules with rings. These pins were typical of the Western Bulgarian lands. In the Sofia region pins, with heads made in the form of a hollow, openwork sphere with a large curved hook, and freely falling small chains with leaf-like pendants, were widespread. In the 19th and 20th centuries these heavy pins were replaced by lighter ones often decorated with plant motifs and the stylized images of birds; they were sometimes made of openwork filigree. In the region of Toutrakan these pins had a comparatively small hollow sphere as their head, cast in openwork, with small chains hanging from them on which there were small cast crosses, openwork platelets in the form of a half-moon, coins and red or blue beads. These additional decorative elements are quite unambiguous proof of the predominant function of this piece of jewellery as an amulet. In the Razgrad region the pins were cast in the particularly characteristic stylized form of a cockerel, with freely hanging

36
Tepeluk, South Bulgaria, 19th century

37
Tepeluk, South Bulgaria, 19th century

36

37

38

39

40

chains on which there were round ornamented pendants and also red and blue beads on the cockerel's tail. This piece of jewellery probably served as an amulet, along with its utilitarian and decorative function, all the more so as here, too, an old Slav or mediaeval Bulgarian tradition had come into play. The *pribodki,* as these pins were called in the Thracian Lowlands, also had as heads small and slightly flattened hollow spheres, cast in openwork and ornamented with a cast imitation of filigree work. To them were attached two slightly longer chains with diamond-shaped pendants and a small hook at the end, from which shorter chains hung freely with cast platelets in the form of a half-moon as pendants. These same short chains were attached to the head of the pin. *Koureshnitsa* was the name of the pin worn in the Rhodope region; it was rectangular, its upper edge cut in the shape of an arc. The upper part of the surface was ornamented with multi-coloured glass stones, granules and a border of filigree flowerets welded onto it. The lower part had platelets thickly placed like fish scales, cut in the shape of a trefoil with an incised 'bird's eye' (a single or double circle with a dot in the middle); this ornament was known in Bulgaria from the Hallstatt Age, and was widespread in the Middle Ages. It had the magic sense of an eye which guarded the owner against the evil eye, or of a sun symbol, which brought good luck. The separately cast rotating rosette with a small stone in the middle, additionally attached in the centre on the thickly arranged scale-like trefoils, can also be accepted as a swastika symbolizing the sun. Filigree flowerets were welded along the end platelets as a border. Certain late 19th century pins, widespread in the regions of Vratsa and Vidin, were made in openwork filigree. Some of them had a round ornament at their

38
Pendant for a kossichnik, South Bulgaria, 18th-19th century

39
Pendant for a *kossichnik,* Karlovo region, 18th-19th century

40
Pendant for a *kossichnik,* Western Bulgaria, 19th century

41

42

43

41
Pendant for a *kossichnik,* South-Western Bulgaria, 19th century

42
Podbradnik the Rhodopes, 19th century

43
Podbradnik, South Bulgaria, 19th century

tops, similar in form and technique to the ornamentation on the *arpalii* earrings. They had an openwork border to which three short chains ornamented with round pendants were attached. Some of the other filigree pins were shaped like a twig of blossoms with decoratively curved leaves and filigree rosettes worked in relief. The *tepeluk* is a round ornamented platelet, embossed in the centre and sewn to a woman's hat in the form of a Turkish fez. *Tepeluks* were wrought or cut out in openwork. The name of this jewel is of Turkish origin (*tepé*=hill), and its use on hats like fezzes points to its Eastern origin. After its Eastern form was accepted, it soon began to be used in the traditional Bulgarian way of life as a Bulgarian jewel. That was why it quickly turned into a Christianized amulet on which iconographic compositions were also wrought, most often the image of St George and the dragon. Pendants with ornaments and amulets were hung on some *tepeluks;* they were pagan symbols used by the Slavs in the Bulgarian State before the Adoption of Christianity as the official religion. In the 19th century *tepeluks* were chiefly made with embossed plant ornaments: some had rosettes in relief in their centres, surrounded by a border of overlapping circlets; others had a large rosette in relief in the centre surrounded by a border of plant ornaments with decorative elements borrowed from West European artistic styles.

Pendants, attached to the hair at the back were typical of certain bridal headdresses, chiefly in Southern Bulgaria. These pendants were formed of several platelets cast in decorative forms and ornamented with a cast imitation of *cloisonné* enamel or filigree welded on. Coloured semi-precious stones or glass and also beads were used in the ornamentation as additional decorative

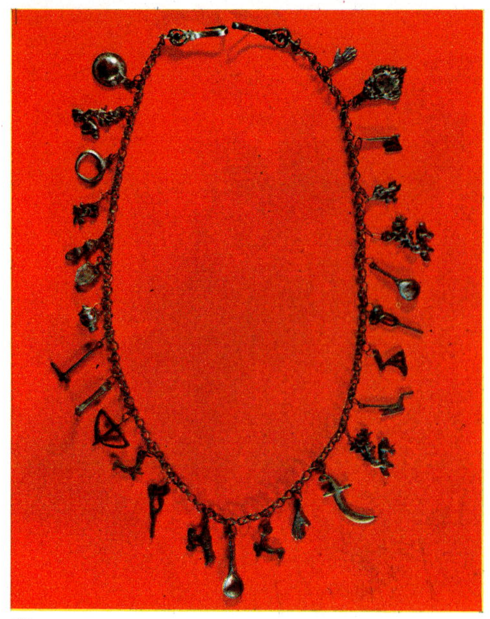

44

45

44
Amulet, South Bulgaria, 19th century

45
Ring, Kotel, 19th century

elements. The platelets were linked by chains, and longer chains with decorative pendants fell freely from the lowest of them. The beauty of these jewels lay in the proportioned structure of the individual elements, as well as in the fine workmanship of the decorative composition.

Podbradniks made of coins (ornaments worn under the chin) developed into artistically made crafts products. In more recent times they were used to hold in place the hat worn in certain headdresses; however, they were also amulets and had a decorative function. The *podbradniks,* worn in the Rhodope region, were of particular interest. They were sumptuous and strikingly decorated. Both ends of this piece of jewellery had semi-ellipsoid platelets cast together with hooks. Their surfaces were decorated with cast imitations of *cloisonné* enamel. Twelve chains joined the platelets to one another. Near the cast ellipsoid platelets these chains were ornamented with decorative platelets, cut into trefoils and ornamented with incised 'bird's eyes' circlets with a dot in the middle) closely arranged like fish scales. The artistic style of these pendents is like the ornament on the *koureshnitsa* pins worn on the head in this region. Other *podbradniks* consisted of only one chain on which a variety of decorative pendants were hung.

Necklaces were characteristic ornaments worn on the body. They were popular as early as the period of the First Bulgarian Kingdom. Torques were also worn at that time. In old sources torques are defined as a bracelet for the neck. It was also worn by men, but was more often given to them for military prowess. The torque worn by the Bulgarian Tsar Symeon was *tsetava,* i. e. it had round medallions or platelets attached to it in front. It consisted of

46
Necklace, Vidin region, 19th century

46

47
Necklace, North-Western Bulgaria, 18th-19th century

47

48
Necklace, Western Bulgaria, 18-th-19th century

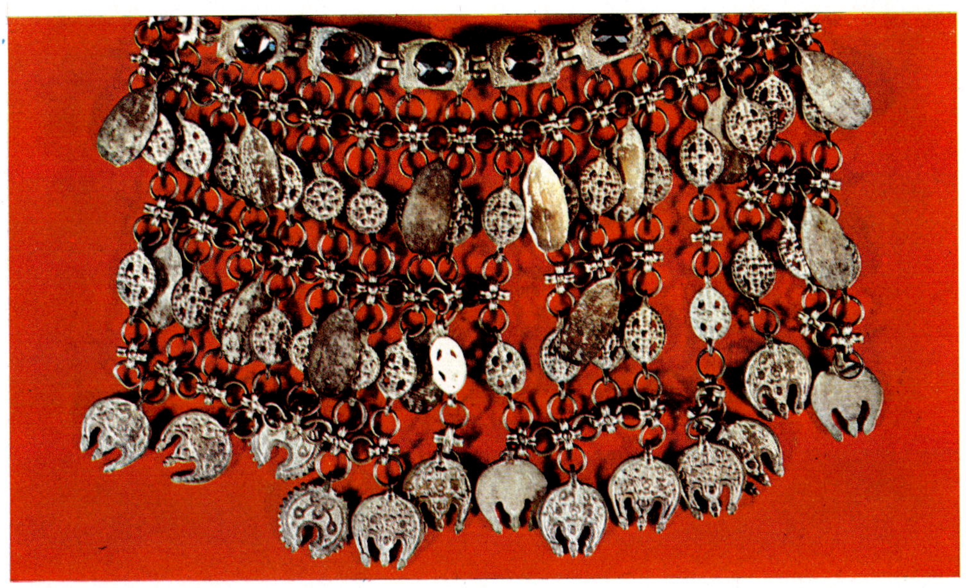

48

a thick circle on which there were three medallions with precious stones inset in them. The boyars also wore torques, but theirs were not mentioned as being *tsetavi.* Silver torques made of two twisted wires were also widespread.

Pendants were also worn in Bulgaria in the Middle Ages; they were usually round, and cast, with an image in relief to serve as an amulet. They were worn on a chain or a string and hung on the breast. After the adoption of Christianity *enkolpion* crosses were widespread, with a hollow middle part in which small pieces of the 'Holy Cross' or 'relics of saints' were placed.

Bulgarian mediaeval jewellery worn on the breast preserved its vitality through the five centuries of Ottoman domination, although its forms and ornamentation did change to a certain extent. Amulet pendants continued to be worn, as necklaces from which various miniature objects hung, such as an axe, a bow and arrows, a cudgel, a yataghan, a spoon, a stag's head, a dog, or a wolf. All these animate or inanimate objects had magic powers of protection, according to the beliefs of the people, and this power was explained by the purpose for which the article was used in ordinary life. Besides the old Slav amulet symbols, some that were typically Moslem were also to be seen, such as the hand of Fatma, Mohammed's mother. Her hand was a protective symbol.

The mediaeval torque preserved its basic form in a woman's piece

49

Necklace, Western Bulgaria, 18-th-19th century

49

of jewellery, worn by a girl engaged to be married, in Kotel and called *halka* (hoop, ring). It was worn in the 19th century and was originally formed of two wires twisted together to form a hoop which was closed in front and fitted around the neck like the old torques. Some 8 or 10 small chains were attached to its front part which had small cast crosses with biconical or palmette-shaped pendants hanging from its lower edge.

In the 18th and the early 19th century necklaces were very widely worn and known by their Turkish name of *gerdan.* Two main variants are to be found among the great variety of their forms and ornamentation: those which fitted closely around the neck, and those which hung down on the breast. Both variants had a variety of pendants hanging from them. The principal part was made of plaited wire, freely linked platelets or cylindrical sections, and in some cases a simple chain. To this main part were attached shorter or longer chains, or freely hung hoops with numerous rosettes arranged vertically along the chains. In some necklaces large round platelets like the medallions of the mediaeval *tsetava* bracelet (torque), were attached to the chains, as well as other decorative pendents, such as the Indian palmette, leaflike, heart-shaped stylized flowers in the style of the widespread Turkish decorative *tulip* style, etc. Almost all these necklaces, which have come down to us, were cast and ornamented with a cast imitation

50
Necklace, Samokov region, 18th-19th century

51
Necklace, Western Bulgaria, 18th-19th century

50

51

52

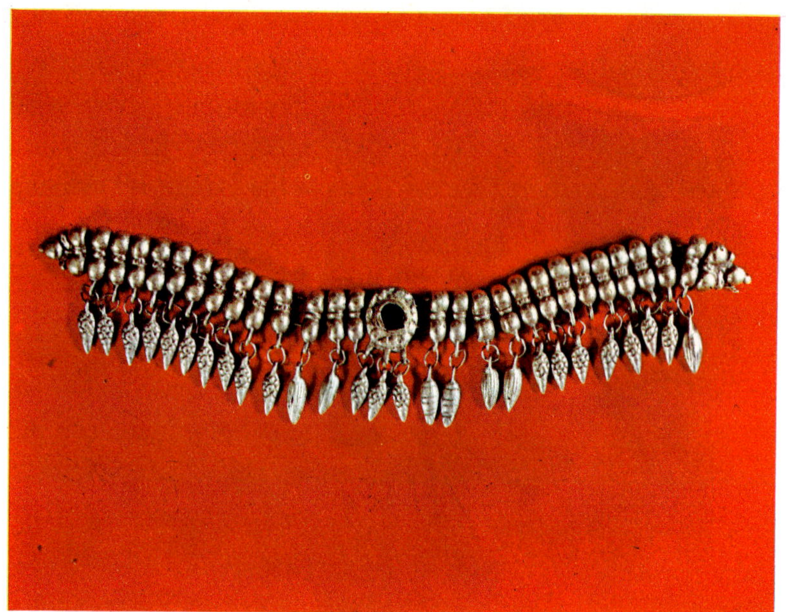

53

of *cloisonné* enamel, but necklaces in real *cloisonné* enamel were probably also made. Semi-precious or glass stones and also gilding, were used as additional ornamentation

Some necklaces, fitting closely around the neck, were formed of small cast ornamented bodies thickly threaded one next to the other on a string, with pendants in the form of a grain of wheat. Some also had a glass stone in the middle. They were known by the name of *kovanez.* Other close fitting necklaces were made of a plaited band with coins hanging from the centre. In the Rhodopes this piece of jewellery was known by the name of *menokero.*

The second type of breast-length necklaces were larger and consisted of one or several small chains with round ornamental platelets attached to them, from which hung small pendants. Some had three rows of chains, with the circles falling one on the other.

Another very lovely piece of jewellery called *kouna* was worn on the breast. It was a characteristic ornament for the new women's costume worn in Kotel region in the 19th century. It consisted of a hexagonal or octagonal platelet, made of mother of pearl or metal, with a religious subject engraved or chiselled on it. It wasmounted in a special nest on another, larger metal platelet and was surrounded by a decorative border of cast small filigree circlets, or another geometrical ornament. Small chains, graded in length and the palmette shaped platelets, circlets and biconical bodies attached to them, form a whole composition with the central platelet. The name of this jewel, *kouna,* was derived from icon, and shows that it did not have merely a decorative place in the costume, but that it was worn as a Christian amulet.

In the period of Ottoman dominationother amulet-pendants were

52
Necklace, South Bulgaria, 19th century

53
Necklace, Chirpan region, 19th century

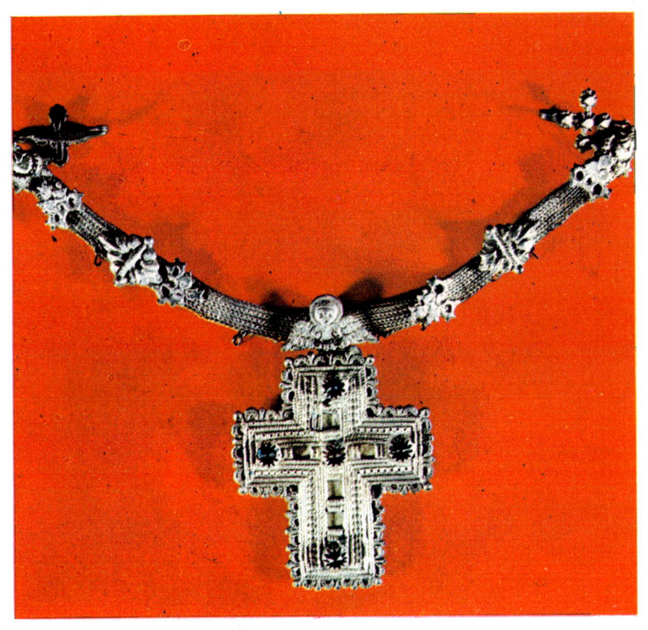

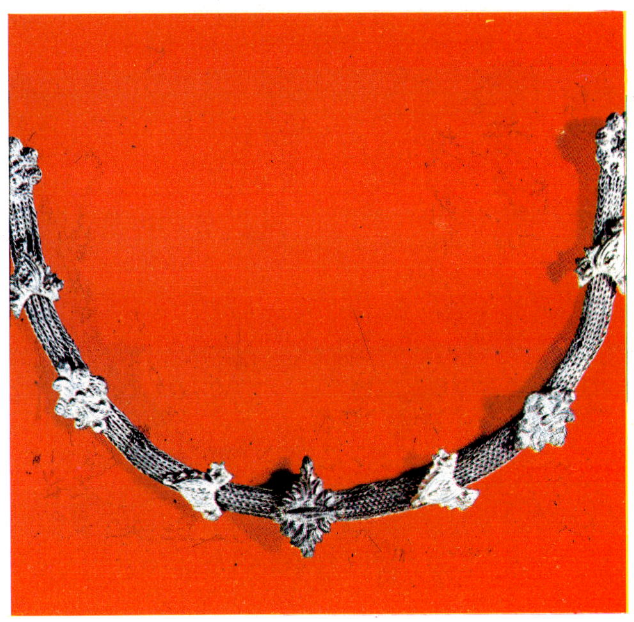

54

Menokero, the Rhodopes, 19th century

55

Small chain from a *menokero,* the Rhodopes, 19th century

also widespread in other regions of the country, together with this Christianized amulet. In South Bulgaria they were in the shape of small triangular or round boxes with images of saints in relief and other symbols, such as a two-headed eagle, characteristic of this period, on the surface. In the Rhodope region these amulet pendants were triangular and were called *mouski.* The *kalemi,* on the other hand, had a small cylindrical box and triangular platelets with decorative pendants on them. The necklaces, in the shape of openwork filigree, made in the Vidin and Vratsa regions appeared comparatively later, at the turn of the 19th and 20th century.

Metal buttons were widely used on mediaeval Bulgarian garments. They were hollow, spherical, unadorned, and had small hoops by which they were sewn on. They were made of silver, copper and bronze, more rarely of gold, being wrought or cast. These buttons were used to fasten front openings and on the lower part of sleeves, between wrist and elbow. Buttons continued to be used during the five centuries of Ottoman bondage, but their form changed to a certain extent, and they became flatter. A typical piece of jewellery was given that name and was widespread in the South-Western Bulgarian lands; however, it was not used to fasten a garment with buttonholes, but, like the fibulae of old, it fastened the front opening of the shirt or chemise by means of small hooks. Basically, these buttons were shaped like palmettes, rosettes, or a round cast platelet with two small hooks on the back. Small chains with decorative pendants were attached to both ends.

During the National Revival period in certain regions where the goldsmiths' craft was widespread, such as those of Stara Zagora and Thrace, certain metal jewels worn on the back and called

56

57

56
Necklace, Kotel, 19th century

57
Necklace, Kotel, 19th century

silver *'gaitani* (braids) were popular. They were close to *kossichniks* in form. They had as a base an ornamented triangular platelet with short chains ending in pendants along the lower edge and hanging down freely; two more long chains with pendants ended in a hook. The platelet was sewn to the hip and the hook was attached to the shoulder.

Metal belts also belong to this group of jewellery. They were worn very widely in Bulgaria during the Middle Ages. This tradition was continued during the period of Ottoman domination. The metal platelets which formed them showed great variety, certain foreign influences being also apparent along with the traditional local forms. After undergoing changes, some types became traditional and were worn until quite recently.

Some belts, entirely made of metal platelets, joined to one another without being strung on a leather strap, have come down to us. They go back to about the 16th century and were typical of North-Western Bulgaria. Leather belts studded with metal platelets were more widespread and in the last century there were even some decorated only with metal studs. In some cases the plateles were sewn onto a leather belt, not rivetted. Among these belts some are to be found consisting of openwork, cast rectangular bronze platelets, with images of saints and other religious motifs by way of decoration. The figures were engraved after casting, but were treated roughly and schematically. Belts of this kind are finished at one end with an oblong bronze platelet, rounded at the end, with palmettes and semi-palmettes, in the Eastern style and decorated with multi-coloured stones.

Besides belts with square platelets, others often found here were studded with narrow metal strips, ornamented in different ways, or

58

59

58

Necklace, South Bulgaria, 18th-19th century

59

Necklace, Vidin, 19th century

else these strips were threaded onto the leather belt. Belts with platelets and buckles ornamented with a cast imitation of *cloisonné* enamel and large in size were particularly impressive. They were often gilded. They were typical of Southern Bulgaria. Certain belts had singly or doubly broken up sections, closely strung beside one another. Some of the sections were decorated with cast granulation. Most of the belts were fastened with a hook and eye, hidden by a platelet in various decorative forms which served to cover the fastening. Semi-precious stones and glass were used as additional decoration. The sections of some of the belts had plant ornaments embossed on them. Filigree examples are comparatively more recent, and began to be made in openwork filigree about the end of the 19th century. They were made of pure silver and were composed of rounded rectangular sections, joined together by tiny little rings. They were fastened by a filigree buckle in the form of a bow. These belts were made in the style of the late Baroque tradition.

Buckles were widely worn in the period of Ottoman domination. They were typical of the traditional women's costumes with which belts were worn. In Bulgaria buckles were found, although comparatively more rarely, as early as the Middle Ages. They were lance- or leaf-shaped with a slightly convex surface, and were decorated with stylized plant motifs in relief.

The great variety of buckle forms in the National Revival period can be reduced to three basic types: oblong with rounded ends, round buckles and buckles in the form of an Indian palmette. Oblong buckles had a very old tradition in mediaeval belt ends. Certain 18th century models were ornamented with a cast imitation of *cloisonné* enamel. They were formed of two or four platelets joined with hinges. Buckles with openwork cast platelets, decorated with a cast imitation of openwork filigree, gilded and set with carnelians, were also widespread in the Sredna Gora region. They were fastened with a hinge. Some buckles in South-Western Bulgaria had oblong and curved side platelets joined by a large rounded platelet like an ellipse in form in the middle. They were wrought in low relief with a stylized plant ornament. Although comparatively more rarely, as early as the 18th century, rectangular buckles with arc-shaped side pieces were found; they were decorated with appliquéd openwork filigree and enamel rosettes in the middle.

Round buckles were usually lance-shaped or had arc-shaped side pieces added to them. Some round buckles were like a rosette or had a decoratively cut out leaf form. The decoration of this type of buckles was most often embossed, with wrought openwork and openwork filigree. Western European influences were particularly strong in their ornamentation. Baroque borders in relief, surrounding a vase, a bunch of flowers or another ornamental motif, were characteristic of many of the embossed buckles. Others were embossed in low relief and had a stylized plant border, and in the centre there was an intricately shaped rosette. Some of the most expensive and artistically worked buckles of the National Revival period were decorated with appliqué openwork filigree surfaces. Among the finest were the so-called *koubelii* and *bourmalii chaprazi* (buckles) made in the centres of the goldsmiths' craft in the Sredna Gora region. Filigree rosettes (*koubeta,* hence *koubelii)* in relief were appliquéd on the flat filigree surfaces,

60
Necklace, South Bulgaria, 18th-19th century

61
Kouna, breast ornament, Kotel, 19th century

62
Necklace, South Bulgaria, 19th century

60

61

62

giving life to the filigree composition as well as playful lightness and exquisiteness.

Buckles, shaped like palmettes, were widespread and offered a great variety of ornamentation. Some of them were shaped like a curly palmette with the tree of life embossed in the middle. Other buckles had a rosette or a strawberry and twigs in their centres. Most of the palmette-shaped buckles had chiselled mother-of-pearl, bone or embossed metal platelets in special palmette-shaped mounts. They were surrounded by a wrought plant border, or one worked with the technique of openwork filigree, or filigree that was welded on. The joining platelet of some of the palmette-shaped buckles with embossed ornaments was made of openwork filigree, the airy convolutions of which gave movement and lightness to the wrought relief of the main platelets.

Buckles were worn by married women,but in the National Revival period buckles for girls also began to be made in the goldsmiths' centres of the economically developed regions. They were made of silver alloys, bronze or brass, most often cast. Leaf-shaped forms or various local decorative variants of the shell type in the Rococo style were often met with.

In the Middle Ages copper, bronze or iron rings were widespread among the population, while gold, and silver ones, ornamented with engravings, filigree, incrustation or settings of precious stones, glass or pearls were worn by the feudal aristocracy.A hoop with an oval or flat cross-section was the most usual and widespread type. During the whole period of the Middle Ages rings, the upper part of which were in the form of an ellipse, a round , a rectangle or a diamond shape were typical; they often

63
Amulet pendant worn on the breast, South Bulgaria, 19th century

64
Mouska from the Rhodopes, 19th century

63

64

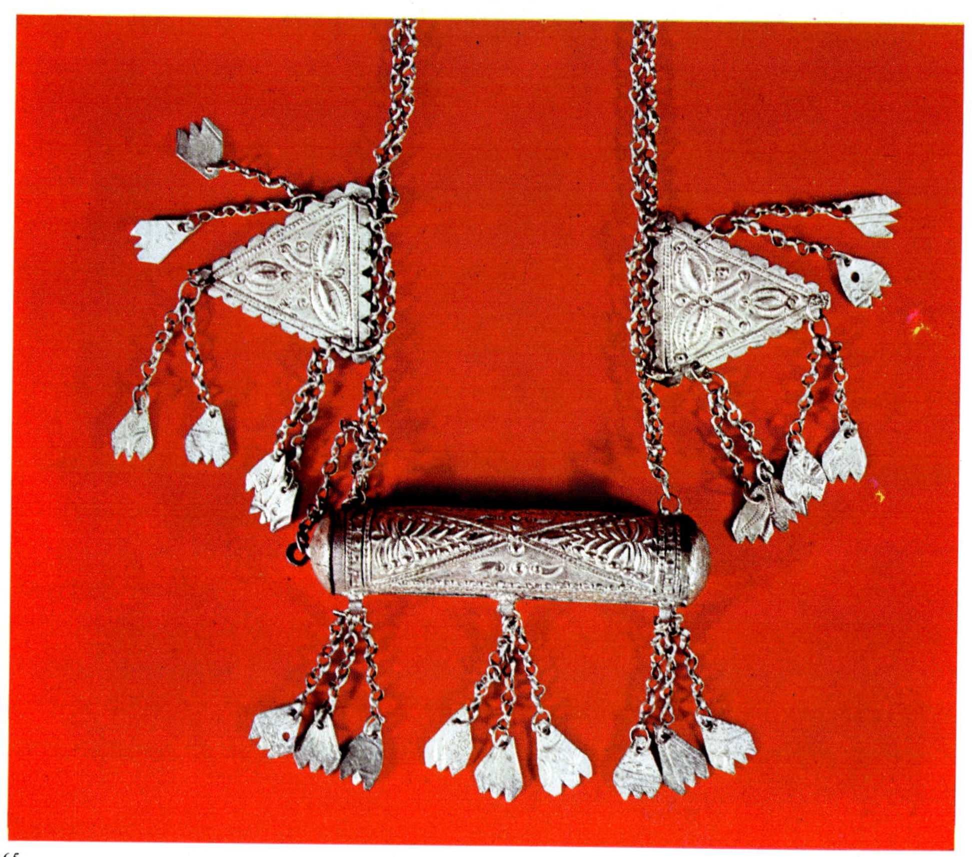

65

had incised geometrical, zoomorphic or plant ornaments. The rings which had a triangular widening at the top were used in shooting with a bow, and served to protect the thumb from the arrow which was being shot. Some of the rings had a platelet welded on to the upper part. In this period one ring was usually worn on the left hand, but seal rings were found on the right hand in necropolises. They were usually cast of massive gold with inscriptions engraved in a negative, and also some other images. Rings were worn by men and women in the period of Ottoman domination as well as during the National Revival. Rings which had images engraved on the platelets were imitations of the intaglios of Antiquity. Rings known in folk songs as *stolovati* rings were widespread in the period of bondage. They developed in Bulgaria from the rings with round platelets. These rings were cast in several parts. A hollow, cylindrical body was welded onto their hoops. Their top platelet was ornamented with rosettes in relief or stars with many rays, surrounded by cast granules. A *groshovat (grosh-like* from *grosh,* a Turkish coin) ring had a round platelet of the same dimension as the Turkish *grosh.* It was ornamented with cast starlike elements. The Kotel girls wore rings called *kantashlii* with a round platelet ornamented in the middle with a red or green glass stone. The filigree rings of more recent times were in the form of a convex rosette.

65
Kalemi mouska from the Rhodopes, 19th century

66

67

66
Kopché breast ornament, Pirin region, 19th century

67
Sreburni gaitani (Silver braids), Thrace, 19th century

Bracelets the ends of which were in the shape of stylized snakes' heads, also used in more recent times, were an old traditional form, inherited from Antiquity. In that period, bracelets were worn on the upper part of the arm, above or below the elbow, in contrast to the Middle Ages, when the new forms of clothing, chiefly the wearing of long narrow sleeves, led to a new wearing of bracelets, above the wrist, like a cuff, forming a finish for the garment. Mediaeval metal bracelets were made of bronze, copper, iron and more rarely of silver and gold. According to data obtained from necropolises, they were worn singly or several together, chiefly on the right arm. Bracelets, made of three or four wires twisted together, with open ends, finished with tabs, were widespread. Another variant of these bracelets was made of six or seven wires twisted together, the ends formed of metal platelets with rounded angles. These ends were ornamented with granules or filigree. The form of a Slav type of braided or twisted bracelet was combined in them with Proto-Bulgarian traditions of decoration,typicalof the ornamentation of belt ornaments. In the period of Turkish feudalism the *koubelii* bracelets developed from them. They were particularly impressive and were worn with traditional festive costumes. *Koubelii* bracelets were open and consisted of three cast hollow parts. The middle part was slightly convex, and the side parts were widened in the shape of a horseshoe. The joins of the pieces were ornamented by a rosette in relief. These bracelets were generally ornamented with arabesques. The widened curved parts were often ornamented with beading, cast together with the whole upper part of the bracelet, since its under part was cut out of a wrought platelet and welded on afterwards. The middle part of some of the bracelets of this type was not ornamented with any special design, but only furrowed with slanting lines in broad or narrow stripes. In some cases a small cross or rosette was placed in the centre. These bracelets were mostly ornamented with cast imitations of *cloisonné* enamel, blue and green enamel being preferred as colours. Gilding was also used by way of additional decoration.

Closed bracelets consisted of two or more parts. Two-part bracelets were in most cases shaped like an ellipse, the parts being joined by hinges, and the fastening also being a hinge. The two parts of these bracelets were embossed or cast.They were often ornamented with one large rosette in the middle with leaves on both sides. Other two-part bracelets with two embossed or cast parallel strips were also widespread and were ornamented with an incised plant design. Several twisted wires were welded onto the edges of the bracelet and between the two convex strips.

Closed bracelets were also made of three or more parts. Three-part bracelets with meandering filigree borders welded onto them and convex small cone-shaped bodies, like thorns, are of special interest. Small rings hung from the places where the separate parts were joined by hinges. These little rings were placed more closely to one another in another variant of these bracelets which had narrow, open-work cast platelets joined by hinges. Glass stones were often found on them, and mercury gilding was used

68

Belt, Provadia region, 18th-19th century

68

69
Belt, South Bulgaria, 18th-19th century

69

70
Belt, South Bulgaria, 18th-19th century

70

71
Belt, Thracian Lowlands, 19th century

71

72

72

Belt, South Bulgaria, 19th century

73

73

Belt, North Bulgaria, 19th century

74

74

Belt, Vratsa region, 19th century

75
Buckles, Western Bulgaria, 18th-19th century

76
Buckles Western Bulgaria, 18th-19th century

on both variants. The first was typical of Teteven goldsmiths, and the second, of the work of Kotel goldsmiths.

In the National Revival period bracelets consisting of five square openwork embossed or cast platelets with plant ornaments in the Baroque style were also widespread. Another well-known type of bracelets worn at this time were known as *enteshii;* they consisted of two rectangular platelets ornamented in various ways, most often with filigree work, and linked together by numerous small chains, some of which had filigree flowerets on them.

An older variety of closed bracelets than those described so far were made of a broad plaited strip, like the plaited necklaces. They were fastened by a hinge, hidden by a rectangular platelet, with others in the shape of ellipses on both sides. The platelets were embossed in low relief in a stylized plant design.

About the turn of the 19th and 20th centuries bracelets made of rectangular, slightly curved filigree sections came into fashion. They were fastened with hinges. They were made of pure silver and often gilded.

Many of the pieces of jewellery described still had a certain practical and utilitarian use in more recent times. The head pins, for instance, held the head scarves to the head; the *podbradniks* kept the hats of the bridal headdresses in place. Buckles fastened belts and the larger ones protected the woman's abdomen when she was engaged in hard work in the fields. The symbolical ornamentation on the buckles, so often met with, in the form of biblical compositions in relief, human and animal figures, plant motifs, etc., which were thought to have the magic power of deflecting evil looks and evil spirits, led to the idea that along with their practical purpose, buckles were worn as Christianized amulets.

Jewellery continued to be involved in many rites and customs, accompanying man from the cradle to the grave. In many places a mother's jewels were placed at the head of her new-born baby. This was done on the third evening when the weird sisters were expected. In Western Bulgaria the mother's buckles had to be placed beside the infant at all costs, together with her other jewels. Several days after birth a baby girl's ears were pierced and after a time small silver earrings were put through them. If a young married woman's babies died at birth, only the right ear of a

77

Buckles. Western Bulgaria, 18th-19th century

78

Buckles, Sredna Gora region, 18th-19th century

79
Buckles, South Western Bulgaria, 19th century

79

80
Buckles, Karlovo region, 18th-19th century

80

81
Buckles, Western Bulgaria, 18th-19th century

81

82

82
Buckles, South Bulgaria, 19th century

83

83
Buckles, Plovdiv, 18th-19th century

baby boy was pierced, and he wore one earring, which he was not supposed to remove even when he grew up to be a man. The earring could only be removed after he reached the age of 50. The same thing was done to a baby boy born on the the same day of the same month on which a child which had died had been born. Rings played a part in the custom called *ladouvané* (singing to the rings). The girls dropped their rings, tied to nosegays, into a small water-filled copper, and took them out one by one while they sang, so as to foretell the future. On St George's day the bride milked the first ewe through a ring so as to guard the sheep against the evil eye and to have them yield a lot of milk during the summer. A ring, called *menovnik,* played an important part at engagements and weddings. A young man gave the girl of his choice a ring and if two rivals wanted the same girl and one of

84
Buckles, Karlovo region, 19th century

84

85
Sahani (dish) buckles, Panagyurishte region, 19th century

85

them had given her a ring and the other a nosegay, the girl would go to the one who had given her a ring. A ring was given at the engagement or the wedding, together with the remaining jewels, among wich there had to be a *prochelnik and* buckles. In most regions of the country the young man gave his future bride all the jewels worn with the local woman's costume at his engagement or the wedding. The ring was also placed in the water in which the new-born baby was bathed. When spells were cast against the evil eye or an evil meeting a bride's ring was taken, because it was believed that it had magical preventive power and could defeat the evil eye. A ring accompanied a dead person on his way to the 'other world', because it was believed that it would help him on his journey. If a ring was dug out of a grave, it was used to treat diseases and particularly to stop nose bleeding; it was placed un-

86

87

der the nose so that the drops of blood could pass through it. On St. George's Day girls and young brides, dressed in their new costumes and wearing their metal jewellery, mixed the dough for the ritual St George's Day bread.

Metal jewellery also played the part of a social regulator in the people's way of life. Thus, for instance, the jewellery worn by a girl, particularly on her head, was far more modest than that of a bride. Buckles in most places were only worn by married women, and when they began to be worn by girls too in the economically more developed regions, they were differentiated by the material they were made of, their form and ornamentation, from those worn by the brides and married women.

As the metal jewellery made by craftsmen became more widespread among the population, it gradually began to take on some of the functions of the objects of folk art produced in the home. While in the pre-National Revival period embroideries and certain other elements of traditional costumes provided the basic signs of belonging to a definite village or hamlet, or else indicated age or family status, as the craft and products of the goldsmiths developed, these functions were gradually taken over by the artistically made craftsmen's jewellery, but no longer in the narrow confines of a village, but on a wider territorial basis. In this period, the aesthetic functions of jewellery were also enhanced. This explains their marked decorative character and the extensive use of elements of the Western European artistic styles in ornamenting them. Jewels were some of the essential indicators of material affluence, but the democratic nature of the class structure in our country during the National Revival period was reflected in the aspect of the jewellery of this period.

86
Detail of buckles, Panagyurishté region, 19th century

87
Buckles, Sliven region, 19th century

88

89

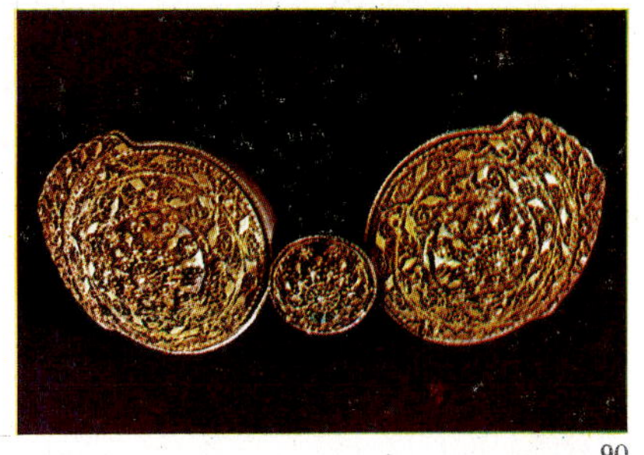
90

91

92

93

88
Buckles, Karlovo region, 19th century

89
Buckles, Karlovo region, 19th century

90
Buckles, Panagyurishté region, 19th century

91
Buckles, Panagyurishté region, 19th century

92
Buckles, Karlovo region, 19th century

93
Buckles, South Bulgaria, 19th century

94
Buckles, South Bulgaria, 19th century

95
Buckles, South Bulgaria, 19th century

94

95

96

97

96
Buckles, South Bulgaria, 19th century

97
Buckles, Pirdop region, 19th century

Social, economic and cultural development during the National Revival period gradually led to the disappearance of most of the luxurious, but unpractical and sometimes unhygienic jewellery which ornamented the head and breast. Up to a time some of it was preserved as ritual jewellery, and later was completely abandoned.

After the Liberation from Ottoman bondage and in the first decades of the 20th century, traditional Bulgarian jewellery, together with the national costumes, became part of the artistic heritage of the past. Museums have preserved certain examples for the coming generations, while the old women in the villages still keep much of the jewellery which they wore in their youth. There will be a flash of silver from a jewel, tucked away in the folds of the *soukmans* and aprons in the chests; it has preserved the vitality and intransience of a tradition of a thousand years which is passing today into the modern jewellery worn by Bulgaria women.

98

98
Buckles, Kotel region, 18th-19th century

99
Buckles, Kotel region, 19th century

100
Buckles of the *koubeliya chaprazi* type, Panagyurishte, 19th century

99

100

101

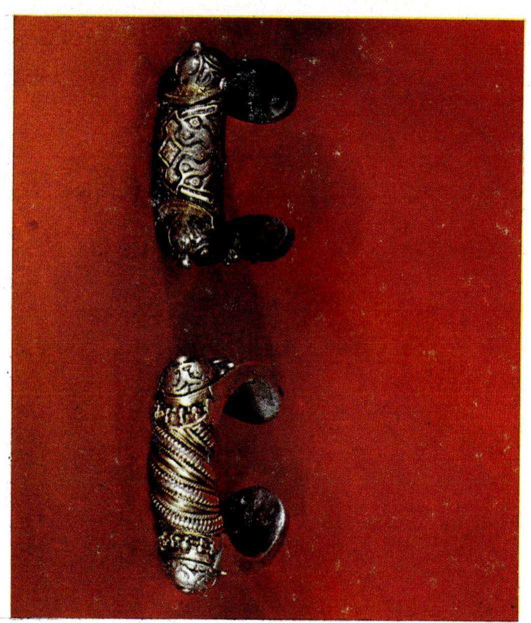
102

103

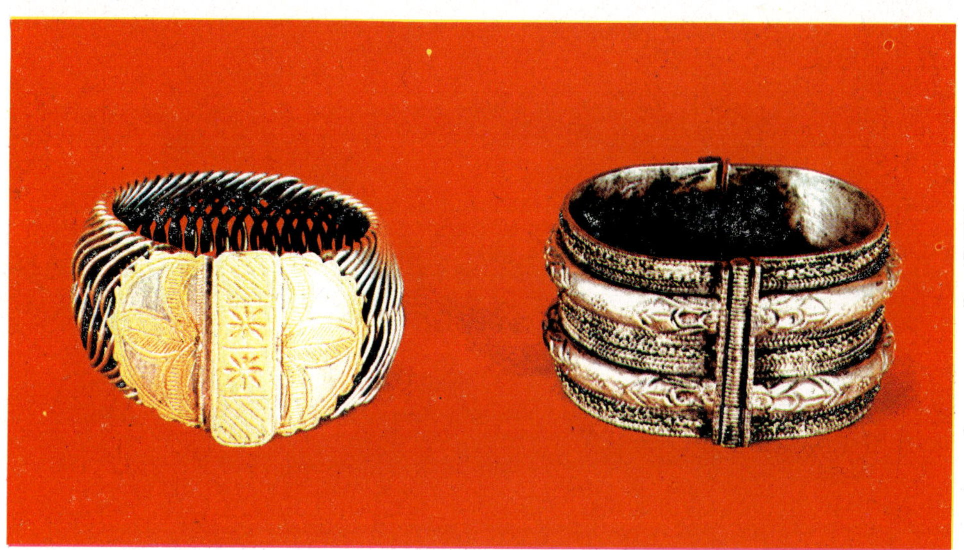
104

101
Mediaeval bracelets from different parts of Bulgaria

102
Boukalii bracelets from diffrent parts of Bulgaria

103
Bracelets, Teteven region, 18th-19th century, Kotel region, 19th century

104
Bracelets, South Bulgaria, 19th century

105

106

107

105
Rings from various parts of the country, 18th-19th century

106
Rings, 19th century

107
Bracelet, Samokov, 19th century

108
Bracelet, Plovdiv, 19th century

108

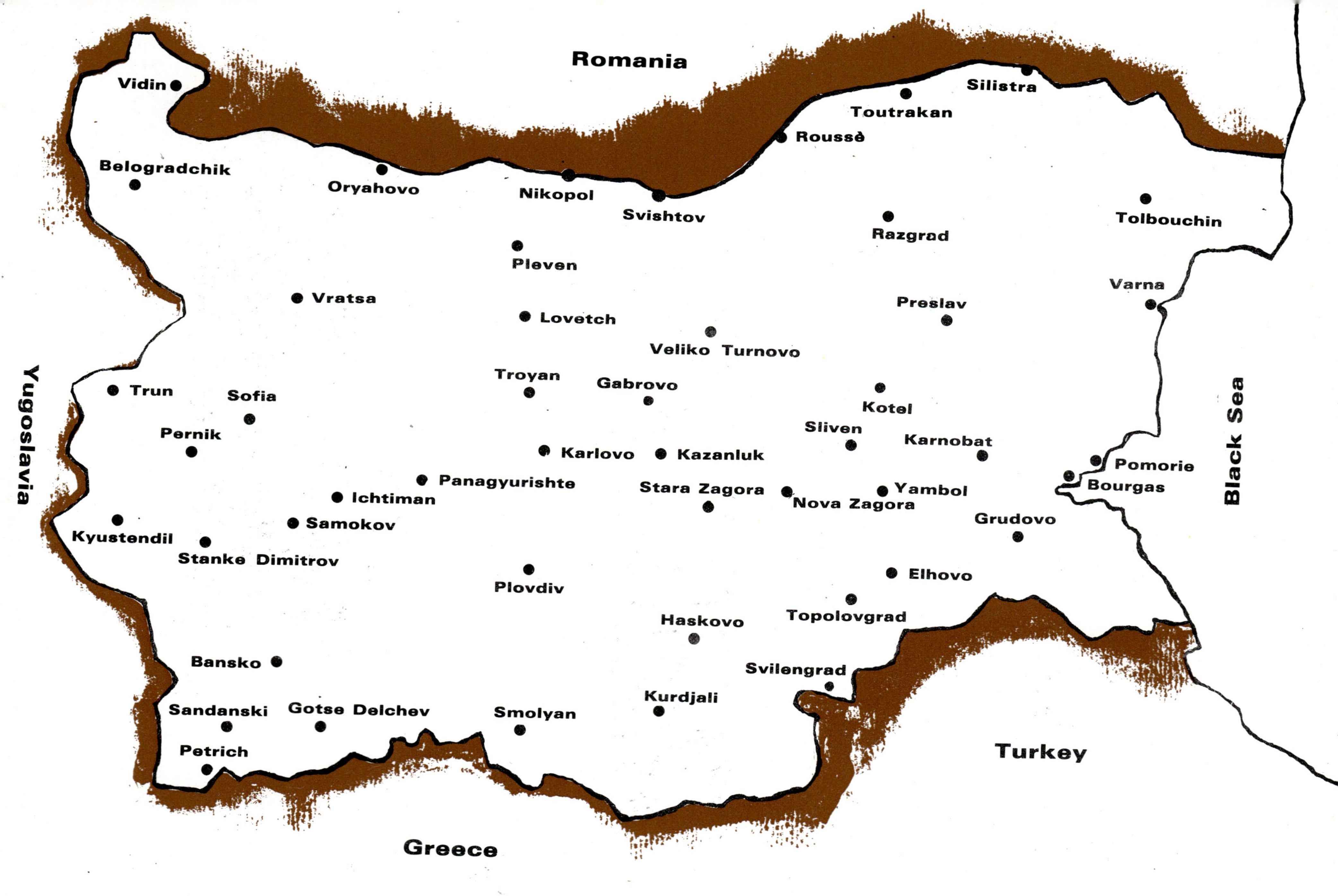

Romania
Vidin
Silistra
Toutrakan
Roussè
Belogradchik
Oryahovo
Nikopol
Svishtov
Tolbouchin
Razgrad
Pleven
Vratsa
Lovetch
Varna
Preslav
Veliko Turnovo
Troyan
Gabrovo
Kotel
Yugoslavia
Trun
Sofia
Pernik
Sliven
Karnobat
Karlovo
Kazanluk
Pomorie
Bourgas
Black Sea
Panagyurishte
Stara Zagora
Yambol
Nova Zagora
Ichtiman
Samokov
Grudovo
Kyustendil
Stanke Dimitrov
Elhovo
Plovdiv
Topolovgrad
Haskovo
Bansko
Svilengrad
Kurdjali
Sandanski
Gotse Delchev
Smolyan
Petrich
Turkey
Greece

BIBLIOGRAPHY (Bulgarian National Costume)

A n g e l o v , D., *Obrazouvané na bulgarskata narodnost* (Formation of the Bulgarian Nationality), Sofia, 1971. 419 pages.

A r n a o u d o v , M., *Bulgarski Svatbeni Obredi* (Bulgarian Wedding Rituals), CY ИФФ. XXVIII, 3 1931

A r n a o u d o v , M., *Stoudii vurhou bulgarskite obredi i legendi* (Studies on Bulgarian Rituals and Legends), v.I. Sofia, 1971

B o z h k o v , At., *Bulgarskata istoricheska zhivopis* (Bulgarian Historical Painting), Sofia, 1972, 270 pp.

B r o m l e y , Yu. V., *Etnos i etnographia* (Ethnos and Ethnography), Moscow, 1973, 283pp.

D u j č e v, Iv., *Bulgarsko Srednevekovié* (Bulgarian Middle Ages), Sofia, 1972, 619pp.

G a g e n-T o r n , N.I., *Zhenskaya odezhda narodnoy Povolzhiya* (Women's Clothing of the people of the Povolzhie), Cheboksari, 1960, 227 pp.

G a n d e v , Hr., *Problemi na bulgarskoto vuzrazhdané* (Problems of the Bulgarian National Revival), Sofia, 1976, 856 pp.

H i n k o v a, H., *Putepisni izvori ot XV i XVI vek za bita i koultourata na Bulgarskiya narod* (Travel Notes of the 15th and 16th century on the Life and Culture of the Bulgarian People), C6HY, No 55, Sofia, 1976, p.145-273

I v a n o v , Yord., *Oblekloto na starité Bulgari* (The Clothing of the Old Bulgarians), *Rodina,* year III, No III, Sofia, 1941, p. 1125

K a t s a r o v , G., *Bitut na starité traki spored classicheskite pisateli* (Way of Life of the Ancient Thracians according to Classical Writers, C6, БАН,No I, 1912, p. I-72

K o y e v , Iv., *Bulgarskata vezbena ornamentika* (Bulgarian Embroidered Ornamentation), Sofia, 1950, p.169

K o s t o v , St. L., *Bulgarski narodni shevitsi* (Bulgarian Folk Embroideries) Part I, Sofia, 1929

K o s t o v , St. L. and Peteva, E., *Bulgarski narodni shevitsi,* Part II, Sofia, 1929

K o s t o v, St.L., *Sofiyska nossiya (Sofia Costume), HEM No VII. Sofia, 1927, p. 14-26*

K o s t o v, St.L., Trunska nossiya (The Trun Costume), HEM, No VIII-IX, Sofia, 1928, p.

K o s t o v , St. L., *Radomirska nossiya* (Radomir Costume), UHEM, No VIII–IX, Sofia, 1936, 1928, p. 135-147

K o s t o v, St.L. *Belodreshkovtsi v Severozapadna Bulgaria* (The White-Garment Wearers in North-Western Bulgaria), HEM, No X-XI, Sofia, 1930-1931, p. 73-102.

K o s t o v , St. L., *Ostanki ot staroto slavyansko obleklo v Bulgaria. Sb. na IV Congress na slavyanskite etnografi i geografi* (Remnants of Old Slavonic Clothing in Bulgaria. Collection of the 4th Congress of Slav Ethnographers and Geographers), Sofia, 1928, p. 327-332

K o s t o v , St. L. and Peteva, E. *Selski bit i izkoustvo v Sofiysko* (Village Life and Art in the Sofia Region), Sofia, 1935, p. 116-174

M e r t s a l o v a , N. M., *Istoriya kostyuma* (The History of Costume), Moscow, 1972, 198 pp.

M i h a i l o v a , G., *Vuznikvané na vuzrozhdensko zhensko obleklo v Panagyurishté i i Panagyursko* (Appearance of National Revival Women's Clothing in Panagyurishté and its Region).ИЕИМ,No X, 1976, pp. 77-127

Mihailova, G., *Promeni v muzhkata traditsionna nossiya ot raiona na Sushtinska Sredna Gora prez epohata na Vuzrazhdaneto* (Changes in the Traditional Men's Costume in the Region of the Real Sredna Gora in the Epoch of the National Revival), ИЕИМ. No XII 1969, p. 11-144

Mijatev, Kr., *Bulgarskiyat Soukman* (The Bulgarian *soukman), Sp.* БАН *No 7, Sofia, 1960, p.219-264*

Miletitsch, *L., Staroto bulgarsko nasselenié v Severoiztochna Bulgaria* (The Old Bulgarian Population in North-Eastern Bulgaria), Sofia, 1902

Mitova-Dzhoneva, D., *Arheologicheski danni za sélskata nossiya v Severozapadna Bulgaria prez XIV v.* (Archaeological Data on Village Costume in North-Western Bulgaria in the 14th Century), ИЕИ, No III, p.40-56

Niederle, L., *Bit i kultura drevnikh slavyan* (Life and Culture of the Old Slavs), Prague, 1924

Peteva, E., *Shevichni Paraleli* (Embroidery Parallels), ИНЕМ, Year X-XI, Sofia, 1932,p. 103-129

Sefterski, R., *Yamourloukut v Bulgaria* (The *Yamourlouk* in Bulgaria), СбНУ, No 50, p.369-403

Telbizova, M. and Telbizov, K., *Narodnata nossiya na banatskité Bulgari* (The Folk Costume of the Banat Bulgarians), Sofia, 1958, 168 pp.

Todorov, N., *Balkanskiyat grad. XV-XIX v.* (The Balkan Town, 15th-19th Century), Sofia, 1972, 504 pp.

Tretyakov, P.N., *Vostochnoslavyanskie cherti v bitu naseleniya Pridounaiskoi Bolgarii* (East Slavonic Features in the Life of the Bulgarian Population along the Danube), Sov. etn., 1948, No. 2, p.170-183, Moscow

Tsoncheva, M., *Houdozhestvenoto nasledstvo na trakiyskité zemi* (The Artistic Heritage of the Thracian Lands), Sofia, 1971, 259 pp.

Tsvetkova, B., *Frenski putepissi za Balkanité XV-XVIII vek* (French Travel Notes on the Balkans 15th-18th Century), Sofia, 1975, 542 pp.

Vakarelski, Hr., *Bit na trakiyskité i maloaziyski bulgari* (Way of Life of the Thracian and Asia Minor Bulgarians), Sofia 1935, p. 159-226

Vakarelski, Hr. and D. Ivanov, *Bulgarskite narodni nossii sega i v minaloto* (Bulgarian National Costumes Today and in the Past), Sofia, 1942,p. 56-147

Vakarelski, Hr., *Bulgarsko narodno izkoustvo* (Bulgarian Folk Art), Sofia, 1963, 21, p.18

Vakarelski, Hr., *Etnografiya na Bulgaria* (Ethnography of Bulgaria), Sofia, 1974, p.226-257, 764-770

Vaklinov, St., *Formirané na starobulgarskata koultoura* (Formation of the Old Bulgarian Culture), Sofia, 1977,293 pp.

Vassiliev, As., *Ktitorski portreti* (Donor Portraits), Sofia, 160, 273 pp.

Vassiliev, As., *Sotsialni i patriotichni temi v staroto bulgarsko izkoustvo* (Social and Patriotic Themes in Old Bulgarian Art), Sofia, 1972, 152 pp.

Veleva, M., *Bulgarski narodni nossii i shevitsi* (Bulgarian National Costumes and Embroideries), Sofia, 1950, 30, p.95

Veleva, M., *Kotlenskata nossiya* (The Kotel Costume) ИБИМ No I, 1953, p.9-62;No II, 1955,p.8-83

Veleva, M., *Edna bulgarska zabradka* (A Bulgarian Way of Wearing the Head Scarf) in *Ezikovedsko-etnografski izsledvaniya v pamet na akad. St. Romanski* (Linguistic-Ethnographic Studies in Memory of Academician St. Romanski), Sofia, 1960, p.879-703

Veleva, M., Za *proizhoda na edna starinna bulgarska shevitsa sus obshto slavyansko razprostranenié* (On the Origin of an Old Bulgarian Embroidery Design Widespread among the Slavs), No IV, ИЕИМ p. 27-82

Veleva, M,*Bulgarskata dvouprestilchena nossiya* (The Bulgarian Two-Apron Costume), Sofia, 1963,162 pp.

Veleva, M., *Sinteza na etnicheskite elementi v bulgarskoto narodno obleklo* (Synthesis of the Ethnic Elements in Bulgarian National Clothing), ИЕИМ, No VII, 1965,p.65-71

Veleva, M. *Danni ot bulgarskité narodni nossii za nyakoi harakterni cherti na oblekloto na Slavyanite* (Data from Bulgarian National Costumes about Certain Characteristic Features in the Clothing of the Slavs). ИЕИМ, No XI, 1968, p.5-69.

Veleva, M.*Bulgarsikité narodni nossii vuv Iztochnite Rodope. Sbornik Narodostna i bitova obshtnost na Rodopskité bulgari* (The Bulgarian National Costumes in the Eastern Rhodopes. Miscellany, Nationality and Common Way of Life of the Rhodope Bulgarians). Sofia, 1967, p. 57-110.

Veleva,M. *Bulgarskite narodni nossii – pametnitsi na koultournoistoricheskoto razvitié na bulgarskiya narod. Sbornik Purvi kongress na Bulgarskoto istorichesko drouzhestvo*

(Bulgarian National Costumes – Records of the Cultural and Historical Development of the Bulgarian People. Proceedings of the First Congress of the Bulgarian Historical Society. Vol.II, Sofia, 1972, p. 172-174

V e l e v a , M, *Za periodizatsiata v razvitieto na bulgarskité narodni nossii* (On Periodization in the Development of Bulgarian National Costumes). E M, No XV, 1974, p. 5-53

V e l e v a , M, *Bulgarski narodni nossii* (Bulgarian National Costumes). Sofia, 1956, 96 pp.

V e l e v a, M. *Raznoobrazie na Bulgarskite narodni nossii* (Variety of Bulgarian National Costumes), Sofia, 1969, 178 pp.

V e l e v a ,M. and Lepavtsova, Evg. *Bulgarski narodni nossii, t. I. Bulgarski nossii v Severna Bulgaria prez XIX i nachaloto na XX vek* (Bulgarian National Costumes, v.I. Bulgarian National Costumes in North Bulgaria in the 19th and Early 20th Century). Sofia, 1960, 324 pp. 120 Illustrations in Colour, 12 Plates with Sketches

V e l e v a , M. and Lepavtsova, Evg. *Bulgarski narodni nossii, t.II. Bulgarski narodni nossii v Sredna Zapadna Bulgaria i Srednite i Zapadni Rodopi ot kraya na XVIIIdo sredata na XXvek* (Bulgarian National Costumes, v. II. Bulgarian National Costumes in Central Western Bulgaria and the Central and Western Rhodopes from the 18th to the mid-20th Century). Sofia, 1974, 254 pp., 120 Illustrations in Colour, 16 Tables with Sketches and Photos

V e l e v a , M. and Lepavtsova, Evg. *Bulgariski narodni nossii, t. III. Bulgarski narodni nossii vuv Iztochna Bulgaria prez XIX i nachaloto na XX vek* (Bulgarian National Costumes, v. III. Bulgarian National Costumes in Eastern Bulgaria in the 19th and Early 20th century). Sofia, 1979, 331 pp., 180 Illustrations in Colour, 16 Tables with Sketches

V e l e v a , M. and Venedikova, V. *Tukani i tukacheski tehniki v Yugoiztochna i Severozapad-na Bulgaria* (Fabrics and Weaving Techniques in South-Eastern and North-Western Bulgaria). Sofia, 1967,134 pp.

V e l e v a , M. and A. Veleva, *Technologiya i houdozhestveni kachestva na bulgarskité narod-ni textilni proizvedeniya* (Technology and Artistic Qualities of Bulgarian Folk Textile Products), Sofia, 1975, 191 pp.with 66 supplements.

V u z h a r o v a , Zh., *Slavyani i prabulgari* (Slavs and Proto-Bulgarians), Sofia, 1976,447 pp.

Y o n o v ,M. *Nemski i avstriyski putepissi za Balkanité, XV-XVI vek* (German and Austrian Travel Books about the Balkans, 15th-16th Century), Sofia, 1979, 515 pp.

Z a ï m o v a – T u p k o v a, V., *Kum vuprossa za vizantiyskoto vliyanie vurhou bulgarskoto obleklo prez Purvata bulgarska durzhava* (On the Question of Byzantine Influence on Bulgarian Clothing in the Period of the First Bulgarian State) ИИВИ No 2, Year I, 1951

V e l e v a, M. *O proizkhozhdeniya nekotorikh elementov v bolgarskom nationalnom costyume, imeyushchikh skhodstvo s odezhdov drugikh balkanskikh narodov. Aktove na I kongress za naoukité na Balkanité i stranité vuv Yugoiztochna Evropa* (On the origin of certain elements in Bulgarian National Costumes having Similarity with the Clothing of Other Balkan Peoples. Proceedings of the First Congress on the Sciences of the Balkans and the Countries of South-Eastern Europe). Vol. VII, Sofia, 1971, p. 483-488.

BIBLIOGRAPHY (Bulgarian Folk Jewellery)

Sn. Blagoeva, *Kum vuprossa za razvitieto i razprostraneniéto naazhournata filigranna tehnika v zlatarskité tsentrové ou nas prez Vuzrazhdaneto.* (On the Question of the Development and Spread of openwork filigree technology in the goldsmiths' centres of the National Revival Period). First Congress of the Bulgarian Historical Society, 1972, v. II. pp. 281-286.

Sn. Blagoeva, *Bulgariski narodni nakiti* (Bulgarian Folk Jewellery). S. 1977.

Sn. Blagoeva, *Zanayati – Sb. Pirinski krai. Etnografski, ezikovedski i folklorni prouchvaniya* (Crafts – Miscellany, The Pirin Region. Ethnographic, Linguistic and Folklore Studies). In the Press.

Ch. Chervan, *Izkoustvoto na starité bulgarski zlatari* (The Art of the Old Bulgarian Goldsmiths). *Izkoustvo* (Art) a periodical, 1967, No 4, p. 25

Sn. Dancheva-Blagoeva, *Priémstvenost na filigrannata tehnika ot 19 v. v Panagyurishté* (Continuity of the technique of filigree work in the 19th century in Panagyuristé).

Sn. Dancheva-Blagoeva, *Priémstvenost na filigrannata tehnika ot 19 v. v Panagyurishté*(Continuity of the technique of filigree work in the 19th century in Panagyurishté). *ИЕИМ, v. XIII, 1971, pp. 95-126.*

Hr. P. Dermendjiev, *Staroto zlatarstvo v Smolvanskiva krai na Rodopskata oblast* (The Old Goldsmiths' Work in the Smolyan Part of the Rhodope Region). *Izkoustvo,* 1975, No 7, pp. 32-37.

V. Droumev, Bulgarskoto zlatarsko izkoustvo (The Bulgarian Art of Toreutics).S. BAH,1976

J. G. Frazer, The Golden Bough, A Study in Magic and Religion, Vol. I – XII, Third Edition, London, 1907.

S. Georgieva, D. Bouchinski, *Staroto zlatarstvo vuv Vratsa* (The Old Goldsmiths' Work in Vratsa), S. BAH, 1959.

Liselotte Hausmann und Lens Kriss-Kettenbeck, Amulett und talisman, Verlag Georg D. W. Callwey, München, 1966.

M. Ivanov, *Zlatarskité proïzvedenia ot 16-19-v. v mouzeya na Bachkovskiya Manastir* (Works by Goldsmiths Made in the 16th-19th Century, in the Museum of Bachkovo Monastery), S. БАН, 1967, p. 111.

Iv. Koev, *Sustoyanié na prouchvaniyata vurhou narodnoto izkoustvo v Bulgaria* (State of the Studies on Folk Art in Bulgaria), ИЕИМ,VIII, 1965, pp. 55-63. Summaries in Russian and French.

St. L. Kostov, *Amouleti protiv ouroki* (Amulets against the Evil Eye), ИHEM, Year I, 1921, NO ii, pp. 91-112.

St. L. Kostov, *Izobrazhenieto na Sv. Georgi v Bulgarksiya naroden nakit* (The Image of St. George in Bulgarian Folk Jewellery), Miscellany in Honour of Professor L. Miletich, S. 1912, pp. 181-201.

St. L. Kostov, *Parité kato nakit* (Coins as Jewellery) ИNEM, Year III, 1928, pp. 130-139

St. L. Kostov, E. Peteva, *Selski bit i izkoustvo v Sofiysko* (The Peasant Way of Life and Art in the Sofia region), S. 1935

M. O. Kosven, *Ocherki istorii pervobitnoy kulturi* (Outlines of the History of Primitive Cultures), M. 1953, p. 91
Adriana G. Marina, *Bulgarskata Pafta* (The Bulgarian Buckle) *Izkoustvo,* 1968, No 1, p. 29.
D. Marinov, *Gradivo za veshtestvnata koultoura na Zapadna Bulgaria* (Building Materials for the Material Culture of Western Bulgaria), S. 1901, p. 116
D. Marinov, *Zhiva Starina* (A Living Antique), III
N. Mavrodinov, *Starobulgarskoto Izkoustvo* (Old Bulgarian Art), S. 1959
G. Mihailova, *Obleklo* (Clothing), in *Sb. Dobroudja (Etnografski, folklorni i ezikovi prouchvaniva)* Miscellany Dobroudja, Ethnogpraphic, Folkore and Linguistic studies)
G. Mihailova, *Za founktsiyata na narodnata materialna houdozhestvena koultoura vuv obshtestvenata praktika na bulgarina* (On the Function of the Folk Material Artistic Culture in the Social Practice of the Bulgarian) *Sb. Folklor i obshtestvo* (Miscellany, Folklore and Society) p. 106-111.
G. Mihailova, *Sotsialni aspekti na narodnoto obleklo* (Social Aspects of Folk Clothing), *Bulgarska ethnografia,* 1976 No 3-4, pp. 5-23.
L. Miletich, *Stari putouvaniya prez Bulgaria*(Old Journeys through Bulgaria) Miscellany HYH, VI, p. 129
V. Nesheva, *Nakitut v srednevekovniya bulgarski kostyum prez 13-14v.* (Jewellery in the Mediaeval Bulgarian Costume in the 13th-14th centtury), Bulgarska etnografia,197, pp. 111-124.
L. Niederle, *Bit i kultura drevnikh slovyan* (Life and Culture of the Old Slavs), Prague 1924
R. Pesheva-Popova, *Starinni bulgarski naoushnitsi i obetsi* (Old Bulgarian Ear-Covers and Earrings), ИЕИМ, V, pp. 75-134.
E. Peteva, *Bulgarki narodni nakiti,* ch, li ch.`i (Bulgarian Folk Jewellery) part I and Part II) ИНЕМ VI i VII.
St. Stanchev, *Stara traditsia vuv edin naroden nakit* (An Old Tradtition in a piece of Folk Jewellery) Archaeologia, 1962, No 2, pp. 5-11.
L. N. Sternberg, *Ukrasheniya,* (Ornaments) Encyclopaedic Dictionary, Brockhaus and Ephon, 1902, v. 68
D. Stoyanova-Seraphimova, *Monetnata oukrassa v bulgarskiya* naroden zehnski kostyum prez 16-17 v. (Coin Decoration in the Bulgarian Woman's National Costume in the 16th-17th century), Bulgarska etnografia, IV, 1979, No 1, pp. 16-35.
V. Tupkova-Zaimova, *Kum vuprossa za vizantiyskoto vliyanié vurhou bulgarskoto obleklo prez Purvata bulgarska durzhava* (On the Question of Byzantine Influence on Bulgarian Clothing in the Period of the First Bulgarian State), ИИБИ, 1951, No 1-2 p. 298, *et seq.*
Hr. Vakarelski, *Bulgarsko narodno izkoustvo* (Bulgaian Folk Art). S. 1963, p.20
M. Veleva, *Bulgarskata dvou-prestilchena nossiya* (The Bulgarian Two-Apron Costume), C. БАН, 1963, pp. 89-91
M. Veleva, *Za proizhoda na bulgarskiya sokai, vuz osnova na etnografski danni* (On the Origin of the Bulgarian Sokai, on the Basis of Ethnographic Data), ИЕИМ, VI, 1963, p. 160
Sn. Blagoeva, *Kum vuprossa za razvitieto i razprostranenieto na azhournata filigranna tehnika v zlatarskite tsentrove ou nas prez vuzrazhdaneto.* (On the Question of the Development and Spread of Openwork Filigree Technology in the Goldsmiths' Centres of the National Revival Period). First Congress of the Bulgarian Historical Society, 1972, v. II. pp. 281-286.
Sn. Blagoeva, *Bulgarski narodni nakiti* (Bulgarian Folk Jewellery). S. 1977.
Sn. Blagoeva, Zanayati – *Sb. pirinski krai. Ethnografski, ezikovedski i folklorni prouchvaniya* (Crafts – Miscellany, The Pirin Region. Ethnographic, Linguistic and Folklore Studies). In the Press.
Ch, Chervan, *Izkoustvoto na starite bulgarski zlatari* (The Art of the Old Bulgarian Goldsmiths). Izkoustvo (Art) a periodical, 1967, No 4, p. 25
Sn. Dancheva-Blagoeva, *Priemstvenost na filigrannata tehnika ot 19 v. v Panagyurishte* (Continuity of the technique of filigree work in the 19th century in Panagyurishté). XIII,1971, pp. 95-126.
M. Ivanov, *Zlatarskité proizvedenia ot 16-19-v. v mouzeya na Bachkovskiya Manastir* (Works by Goldsmiths Made in the 16th-19th Century, in the Museum of Bachkovo Monastery), S. Ah, 1967, p. III.
Iv.Koev, *Sustoyanie na prouchvaniyata vurhou narodnoto izkoustvo v Bulgaria* (State of the Studies on Folk Art in Bulgaria), EM, v. VIII, 1965, pp.55-63. Summaries in Russian and French.
St. L. Kostov, *Amouleti protiv ouroki* (Amulets against the Evil Eye), HEM, Year I, 1921, No II, pp.91-112.
St. L. Kostov, E. Peteva, *Selski bit i izkoustvo v Sofiysko* (The Peasant Way of Life and Art in the Sofia region), S. 1935 M.O. Kostven, *Ocherki istorii pervobitnov kulturi* (Outlines of the History of Primitive Cultures), M. 1953, p. 91

GLOSSARY

Aba – thick homespun for upper garments; outer garment, usually men's, sometimes women's made of this homespun.

Aladja – striped material, woven of wool, cotton or mixed materials, used for women's upper garments and sometimes also for men; woman's outer garment made of this material, open down the front, with long or more rarely short sleeves.

Altitsi – Insets at the sides of the chemises, from the underarm down to the hem line, give the chemise a flared look.

Anteria – man's upper garment made of woollen or cotton material, sometimes quilted, its fronts meeting or overlapping; woman's upper garment made of smooth plain or multicoloured material, also sometimes striped along the warp, long and with long sleeves; open down the front.

Belki – strips of coloured material, placed perpendicularly to the hem along the bottom of the *soukmans* worn in some parts of Bulgaria.

Benevretsi – Men's tight-legged trousers, usually made of thick woollen cloth, most often white, ornamented with embroidery in white cotton or black braid along the front of the trouser-leg.

Borka – Chemise gathered around the neck or top of sleeves, worn with the two-apron costume in North Bulgaria. Also *burchanka.*

Burchanka – See above. Also *borka.*

Bruchnik – pleated back skirt made, according to the region, of plain blue material with a striped border, or of striped (along the weft) woollen material; it was usually made of two strips of material horizontally joined by a seam, and was tied around the waist. Also known in different regions as a *kurlyanka, peshtemal* and *vulnenik.*

Dimii – Very wide short-legged trousers, gathered or pleated at the waist and worn with gaiters. Usually ornamented with braiding.

Djoubé – man's or woman's jacket, made of thick woollen material, coming down below the waist, open down the front, ornamented with embroideries or fur.

Dolatanka – Outer garment of thick woollen material open down the front, reaching down below the waist, with long or elbow-length sleeves (hence its name, from *lakut elbow).* Ornamented with embroideries or braiding.

Elek - waistcoat, also sometimes worn by women, but chiefly by men. It is made of woollen, cotton or silk material in various colours, and is ornamented with linear embroidery or braiding.

Eminii – hand-sewn men's shallow leather shoes; black or yellow.

Gougla – man's lambskin hat, worn with the fur outside, cylindrical semi-spherical or cone-shaped in form; also hood attached to an outer garment to guard the head from cold and rain.

Gouna – Man's outer garment made of thick woollen material

Gounel – woman's upper garment, similar to a *soukman* in cut, long and tunic-shaped, sleeveless; made of woollen material.
Grizh – summer *soukman,* usually made of white cotton.
Kalpak – man's fur hat.
Kaltsi or Kaltsouni – Leggings worn by men and women, made of thick woollen material, either dyed black or brown, or in the natural colour of the wool ; shaped like boots, coming up to the knees, and braided along the seams and edges.
Kené – Needle-point lace used in joining seams in white or yellow silks, and in colours to make sleeve edgings in a variety of plant and other patterns. Also known as *zarafluk* and *sachak*
Klashnik -- Woman's outer garment, or man's upper garment made of thick woollen material, knee-length, open down the front, with sleeves or sleeveless, close-fitting at the waist and full-skirted, ornamented with braiding along the edges and seams.
Kolchak – An appliquéd stripe along the front of men's trousers used by way of decoration, with additional embroidery and braiding.
Kossichnik – ornament worn over the hair and attached to the back of the head.
Kozhouh – sheepskin jacket, worn with the fur on the inside, decorated on the outside with appliquéd pieces of coloured leather, forming patterns.
Kurlyanka - back skirt of the two-apron costume, worn in North-Eastern Bulgaria. Other back skirts are known as *bruchniks, peshtemals* and *vulneniks.*
Kebe – Woman's or man's outer garment of thick woollen material, knee – or ankle-length, open down the front; thick tufted blanket or rug.
Lapchouni – Ankle-high slippers made of thick woollen material worn at home, or in the shoes or boots when going out.
Manofil – Summer soukman, usually made of white cotton.
Menté – Sleeveless men's or women's outer knee-length garment of thick woollen material, open down the front and ornamented with linear embroidery or braiding along the seams and edges, and particularly at the tops of the insets.
Narukvisti – Arm-covers, from wrist to elbow, knitted or made of warm material.
Navoushta – Puttees of white wollen cloth, made of rectangular pieces of thick woollen material, covering the feet and legs from the toes up to the knee, held in place by leather straps or black woollen cord.
Pig-or Ox-skin Sandals- boat-shaped with a pointed or rounded tip, held to the foot by leather straps or cords, thrust through the sides. Also known as *tsarvouli.*
Peshtemal - back skirt worn with two-apron costume in North Bulgaria. Also known in other regions as *bruchnik, kurlyanka* and *vulnenik.*
Potouri – full-bottom breeches, worn by the men in many parts of the country.
Prochelnik – metal ornament worn by the women on their foreheads over their head scarves.
Sachak – Needle-point lace, also known as *kené* and *zarafluk.*
Saltamarka – Man's or woman's outer garment of woollen cloth, waist-length, open down the front with long sleeves, rarely without sleeves; sometimes ornamented with braiding along seams or edges, or with bands of fur down the front.
Saya – Woman's upper garment made of woollen or cotton material, plain or striped; open down the front with short or long sleeves, rarely sleeveless; ornamented with linear designs around the neckline, the sleeve-ends and partly the skirts.
Shalvari – Baggy trousers worn by the notables, braided along the seams and edges, and particularly richly around the pocket slits; made of woollen material. Worn by Turkish women, made of lighter material.
Tarlitsi – Slippers of woollen material, worn indoors, over which the shoes were worn outside.
Tsarvouli – pig– or ox-skin sandals. See *opintsi.*
Vouliya – Leather bag in which food was carried on journeys or when out grazing sheep or cattle.
Vulnenik – Back skirt worn with two-apron costume in North Bulgaria. Also known in different regions as *bruchnik, kurlyanka or vulnenik.*
Vruvchanki – type of *tsarvouli* (sandals).
Yamourlouk – Shepherd's cape, made of a thick cloth woven in a mixture of wool and goatshair to make it waterproof. It had a hood.
Zarafluk – Needle-point lace, also known as *kené and sachak.*

ABBREVIATIONS

ГСУИФФ	Annual of Sofia University, Department of Philology and History
ИЕИМ	Bulletin of the Ethnographic Institute and Museum
ИИБИ	Bulletin of the Institute of Bulgarian History
ИБИБ	Bulletin of the Bulgarian Historical Museum
ИНЕМ	Bulletin of the National Ethnographic Museum
Сб-БАН	Miscellany – Bulgarian Academy of Sciences
Сб НУ	Collection of Folk Art and Folklore

BULGARIAN NATIONAL COSTUMES
AND FOLK JEWELLERY

Authors MARIA VELEVA, SNEZHANA DANCHEVA-BLAGOEVA
Photos BOGDAN STEPHANOV
Reviewer Prof. IVAN KOEV
Editor: CHRISTINA ATANASSOVA
Translation MARGUERITE ALEXIEVA
Lay-out VENELIN VULKANOV
Art Editor: MIRA BOLGAR
Techn. Editor DIMITAR ZAHARIEV
Proof-reader TSVETANA DISHKOVA

Septemvri Publishing House, Sofia, 1983
Septemvri Printing House